Education Past and Present

Reflections on Research, Policy, and Practice

Edited by

MEGIN CHARNER-LAIRD
MORGAEN L. DONALDSON
SOO HONG

Harvard Educational Review

75th Anniversary Issue

Library of Congress Control Number 2004116557
ISBN 0-916690-45-8

Published by Harvard Educational Review,
an imprint of the Harvard Education Publishing Group

Harvard Educational Review
8 Story Street
Cambridge, MA 02138

Cover Design: Anne Carter
Typesetting: Sheila Walsh

The typeface used in this book is New Baskerville.

Harvard Educational Review

VOLUME 75   NUMBER 1   2005

The *Harvard Educational Review* is a journal of opinion and research in the field of education. Articles are selected, edited, and published by an editorial board of graduate students at Harvard University. The editorial policy does not reflect an official position of the Faculty of Education or any other Harvard faculty.

Editorial and Business Office
Harvard Graduate School
  of Education   TEL: 617-495-3432
8 Story Street, 1st Floor   Within USA: 1-800-513-0763
Cambridge, MA 02138–3752   FAX: 617-496-3584
Email: hepg@harvard.edu
Web site: http://gseweb.harvard.edu/~hepg/her.html
HER Online Subscribers web site: http://www.edreview.org

Douglas Clayton, *Director*
Laura Clos, *Manuscripts*
Wendy McConnell, *Subscriptions*
Alexandra Merceron, *Marketing Manager*
Dody Riggs, *Production Manager*

The *Harvard Educational Review* (ISSN 0017–8055) is published four times a year, in Spring (February), Summer (May), Fall (August), and Winter (November) by the Harvard Graduate School of Education, Harvard University. Editorial and Business Office: Harvard Graduate School of Education, 8 Story Street, 1st Floor, Cambridge, MA 02138-3752. Periodicals postage is paid at Cambridge, MA 02138-3752, and additional mailing offices. Postmaster: Send address changes to Harvard Educational Review, Harvard Graduate School of Education, 8 Story Street, 1st Floor, Cambridge, MA 02138-3752. Subscribers are asked to send the mailing label from their most recent copy when requesting a change of address.

Subscription information: *U.S.:* individuals, 1 year, $59.00, 2 years, $99.00; institutions, 1 year, $139.00, 2 years, $239.00; students (in a degree program), 1 year, $26.00. *Canada:* individuals, 1 year, $79.00, 2 years, $129.00; institutions, 1 year, $159.00, 2 years, $279.00. *All other international:* individuals, 1 year, $99.00, 2 years, $159.00; institutions, 1 year, $179.00, 2 years, $309.00. *Canada please add 7% GST (#129-795-027).* Foreign subscriptions must be pre-paid in U.S. dollars; checks must be drawn on a U.S. bank. Correspondence should be addressed to: *Harvard Educational Review,* Harvard Graduate School of Education, 8 Story Street, 1st Floor, Cambridge MA 02138-3752. Phone: 1-800-513-0763; 617-495-3432. Single and back issue copies: $15.00. Special issues and symposia are priced individually.

Microform is available from University Microfilms, Inc., 300 N. Zeeb Rd., Ann Arbor, MI 48106; telephone 1-800-521-0600.

The *Harvard Educational Review* accepts contributions from teachers, practitioners, policymakers, scholars, and researchers in education and related fields, as well as from informed observers. In addition to discussions and reviews of research and theory, *HER* welcomes articles that reflect on teaching and practice in educational settings in the United States and abroad. Authors can elect to indicate whether they are submitting their manuscript as an article, a Voices Inside Schools article, an essay review, or a book review. **Guidelines for Authors are located at the back of the issue.**

Indexed in the *Educational Index* and *Book Review Index.* Appropriate articles abstracted in *Academic Abstracts, America: History and Life, Current Index to Journals in Education, Educational Administration Human Resources, Family Resources Database, Historical Abstracts, Psychological Abstracts, Research into Higher Education, Social Science Source, Social Work Research and Abstracts, Sociological Abstracts, Sociology of Education Abstracts, United States Political Science Documents,* and *Urban Affairs Abstracts.* Printed by The Sheridan Press, Hanover, PA 17331. Typography by Sheila Walsh, Somerville, MA 02143.

COPYING REGULATIONS

Harvard
Educational
Review

VOLUME 75   NUMBER 1   2005

Preface

In its first volume, published in February 1931, the *Harvard Educational Review* addressed two issues still of great relevance in this celebratory volume, which appears at the start of the journal's seventy-fifth anniversary year.[1] In the opening essay, editor Charles Swain Thomas, arguing for the use of historical and philosophical methods in addition to the scientific method in educational scholarship, asked, "How can we fail to realize that the truth we seek in education must be sought in many ways and seen from many angles?" (1931, p. 4). In his article, contributing author A. Lawrence Lowell observed that education was believed to be "an instrument of equality" whose aim "is the largest opportunity for all to develop their abilities to the highest point" (1931, p. 95).

Continuing this recognition of educational research as an interdisciplinary enterprise, this volume brings together seven renowned scholars from the field. Each scholar comments from his or her own unique perspective on the evolution of educational scholarship during the seventy-five years of *HER*, and on the state of education today. Each author also pays particular attention to the themes of equity and diversity in tracing educational developments to their present state, and in speculating about the future of the field. Thus, in fundamental ways, this 2005 anniversary edition continues the work begun in 1931: to bring an array of respected scholars' perspectives to bear on important issues, such as equity and diversity, that have shaped the field of education.

In what follows, we provide a brief snapshot of a few articles from the *Harvard Educational Review* archives that were in the forefront of the field regarding issues of equity and diversity. As the contributors to this volume assert, many of these past articles and issues remain timely and pertinent in today's educational arena. Given *HER*'s rich history of engaging such issues, we felt it was only natural to highlight issues of equity and diversity in the chapters of this celebratory volume.

The work of the authors in this volume thus mirrors the history of scholarly publishing in the *Harvard Educational Review*. Now entering its seventy-fifth year of publishing educational research, *HER* has presented numerous cutting-edge articles that address issues of equity and diversity. While early issues of the journal dealt predominantly with ideas particular to Harvard University, the journal quickly found itself at the forefront of discussions regarding race, social class, and equity.[2] In 1959, Talcott Parsons addressed the ways schools reinforce social-class divisions. Provoking a conversation that persists in educational circles today, Parsons detailed ways in which teachers, through their everyday actions and choices in the classroom, reproduce existing social structures. By likening a school classroom to a social system, Parsons revealed the powerful sorting and labeling functions that unwittingly, yet frequently, occurred in classrooms of the time. This article, like many that were to come in the *Review*, detailed issues that remain salient in educational policy, practice, and research today. Thus, in looking back through the pages of *HER*, many of the articles serve as much as a call to action today as they did when they were first published.

Issues of social equity, as well as the mechanisms of social reproduction inherent in public schools, were taken up again in 1970 by Ray C. Rist. He argued that, in direct contradiction to the goals of public education as the great equalizer, public schools serve to reify social-class inequality. In the same year, Paulo Freire wrote about the potential of education to liberate adult learners from reproductive social systems. Freire argued that pedagogy that valued learners' experience and knowledge, rather than merely using mechanistic methods, could transform adult literacy education. Freire's argument supports education as a tool for equality and freedom, empowering learners to critique the role of culture in shaping their experiences and, through praxis, to fight for equity and justice.

The release of the Coleman Report in 1966 heralded the beginning of intense examination of race and equity in the pages of *HER* — an examination that continues in full force today. In 1968, the journal published a special issue (copublished with Harvard University Press) reanalyzing the data from the Coleman Report and critiquing its findings. In addition to the articles that called for new policies aimed at addressing the achievement gap, Coleman himself noted a recent shift in conceptions of equality that focused on the equality of educational outputs for students, as opposed to the equality of inputs. This focus rings true today, although couched now in the terminology of standards and accountability.

Lisa Delpit's oft-cited 1988 article pushed the issue of equity further into the curricular domain of the classroom by critiquing pedagogy that failed to recognize the racial and cultural differences among children in U.S. public school classrooms. Her piece began a conversation about the "culture of power" existing in schools and classrooms, and the ways teachers could explicitly empower their students by teaching them to understand the unspoken rules of this culture. This discussion of power and race would be followed by a series of articles in later issues that broadened definitions of race/racism and examined its effects in classrooms and schools. One of these articles, authored by Beverly Daniel Tatum (1992), engaged issues of racial equity by theorizing about racial identity development. Through a discussion of the interaction between race-related content and students' motivation to learn in college classrooms, Tatum described stages of racial identity that could shape an individual's development. This piece provided new ways to think about the racial identity development of all students and the impact that such an understanding can have on pedagogy and student learning.

Just as Delpit's and Tatum's articles helped to expand our understanding of race, identity, equity, and power, Stacey J. Lee (2001) widened the racial discourse in *HER* through an investigation of the experiences of Asian American students. By studying the experiences of Hmong students, Lee revealed a portrait of Asian American students that did not fit neatly into the Asian "model minority" myth perpetuated through much of the educational literature. Instead, she emphasized the importance of considering both cultural and structural forces in the shaping of these students' attitudes toward education, and noted the multitude of educational experiences that can result from the interaction between these two variables. Bryan McKinley Jones Brayboy (2004) also enhanced the discourse in *HER* around issues of equity. His investigation of the experiences of Native American students at Ivy League universities revealed nuanced strategies around visibility and invisibility that these students employed to preserve their sense of cultural integrity and make their voices heard within their college communities. These articles are only a few of the many published in *HER* that have expanded our perspectives on racial equality/inequality in education.

Just as many articles in *HER* have grappled with issues of race and equity, so too has the issue of gender equity played a prominent role in many pieces in the journal. In 1977, Carol Gilligan asserted that Lawrence Kohlberg's stages of moral development did not apply equally to males and females. Instead, Gilligan argued that for women, responsibility and care are central to moral thought and action and intricately tied to their conceptions of self. This article calling for the inclusion of the feminine voice in developmental studies launched a movement within the field of educational psychology that questioned the generalizability of theories of development. Further examining issues of gender, in 1996, Jackie M. Blount took a historical look at the employment patterns of women in education. In spite of the predominance of women in the field of teaching, Blount argued that women who fell outside of traditional gender roles were stigmatized in the field. She traced patterns of gender inequalities, identifying homophobia as the root of many discriminatory practices, particularly in cases where women sought leadership roles, like superintendent. Ultimately, Blount concluded that public education will remain entrenched in traditional gender roles until gay, lesbian, bisexual, and transgender educators are welcomed and valued in the field.

Finally, *HER* has seen the emergence of new conversations regarding equity and diversity within its pages. Tom Hehir's 2002 article on the elimination of "ableism," or the devaluing of disability, in education expanded conversations in the field of special education and disability studies to include considerations of the ways in which ableist assumptions can affect the school experiences of students with disabilities. Like many of the pieces in *HER*, Hehir's presents practical applications of theory as he recommends six practices through which schools can begin to eliminate ableism and provide more equitable and inclusive educational experiences for all students.

As the editors of this special volume, we invited seven authors to participate in this reflective conversation. In their own work, these noted scholars have charted new territory for educational research and pushed the field in new directions — often challenging past traditions and raising issues of equity and diversity in their own work. Representing diverse disciplines and perspectives of inquiry in the field of education, Gary Orfield, Ellen Condliffe Lagemann, Kieran Egan, Sonia Nieto, Jean Anyon, Nelly Stromquist, and Kevin Kumashiro reflect on the expansive, growing, and widely debated field of educational research as it has unfolded over the past seventy-five years. These authors address some of the defining moments of the field, as well as the watershed moments in and outside education that have inevitably shaped the progress of educational research. While these chapters focus on moments from the past, each author remains faithful to the present concerns of education, as well as its possibilities and future directions.

With deep gratitude, we thank the seven authors for the hard work, thought, and passion they have contributed to this anniversary volume. We also thank our fellow Board members at the *Harvard Educational Review*, who worked tirelessly alongside us on this project, providing valuable feedback on manuscripts, thoughtful editorial suggestions, and partnership through each step of the publication process. Finally, thank you to the legacy of authors, Board members, and readers who have helped to shape this journal throughout its lifetime. To the readers of *HER*, we express our hope that educational research over the next seventy-five years and beyond will be as engaging and illuminating as it has been in the years this volume celebrates.

MEGIN CHARNER-LAIRD
MORGAEN L. DONALDSON
SOO HONG
75th Anniversary Issue Editors

Notes

1. The *Harvard Educational Review* was then called the *Harvard Teachers Record*.
2. This, and much of the historical information regarding the *Harvard Educational Review*, is drawn from Michael Schudson's "A History of the *Harvard Educational Review*" (1981).

References

Blount, J. M. (1996). Manly men and womanly women: Deviance, gender role polarization, and the shift in women's school employment, 1900–1976. *Harvard Educational Review, 66*, 318–338.

Brayboy, B. M. J. (2004). Hiding in the ivy: American Indian students and visibility in elite educational settings. *Harvard Educational Review, 74*, 125–152.

Coleman, J. S. (1968). The concept of equality of educational opportunity. *Harvard Educational Review, 38*, 7–22.

Delpit, L. D. (1988). The silenced dialogue: Power and pedagogy in educating other people's children. *Harvard Educational Review, 58*, 280–298.

Freire, P. (1970). The adult literacy process as cultural action for freedom. *Harvard Educational Review, 40*, 452–477.

Gilligan, C. (1977). In a different voice: Women's conceptions of self and morality. *Harvard Educational Review, 47*, 481–517.

Hehir, T. (2002). Eliminating ableism in education. *Harvard Educational Review, 72*, 1–32.

Lee, S. J. (2001). More than "model minorities" or "delinquents": A look at Hmong American high school students. *Harvard Educational Review, 71*, 505–528.

Lowell, A. L. (1931). Democracy, equality, and education. *Harvard Teachers Record, 1*, 94–98.

Parsons, T. (1959). The school class as a social system: Some of its functions in American society. *Harvard Educational Review, 29*, 297–318.

Rist, R. C. (1970). Student social class and teacher expectations: The self-fulfilling prophecy in ghetto education. *Harvard Educational Review, 40*, 411–451.

Schudson, M. (1981). A history of the *Harvard Educational Review*. In J. R. Snarey, T. Epstein, C. Sienkiewicz, & P. Zodhiates (Eds.), *Conflict and continuity: A history of ideas on social equality and human development*. Cambridge, MA: Harvard Educational Review.

Tatum, B. D. (1992). Talking about race, learning about racism: The application of racial identity development theory in the classroom. *Harvard Educational Review, 62*, 1–24.

Thomas, C. S. (1931). Positions. *Harvard Teachers Record, 1*, 3–5.

Introduction

GARY ORFIELD
Harvard Graduate School of Education

When the *Harvard Educational Review* began publishing three-quarters of a century ago, the nation's public schools played a much less critical role in the lives of their students and society than they do today. Public intellectuals, not research scientists, played the most influential role in determining how schools worked. The great majority of students did not finish high school, and college was for the privileged few. There were many jobs that could support a middle-class family for which a formal education was not very important. Race was perceived as mostly a southern problem, and the immigrants who sparked some concern came largely from Southern and Central Europe. Although times were different, the schools were then, as they have been for so many generations, an area of deep interest in American public life and of critical importance to the American ideology of opportunity.

Since that time, the schools' role and the society they serve have undergone considerable transformation, and it is clear that significant changes are far from over. Demographic shifts within the United States, the rise of huge multinational employers, and the integration of the global economy and labor market guarantee that great changes are yet to come. It is well to use the *Review's* diamond anniversary to reflect on what has happened, where we are going, and how we currently understand educational processes and institutions. To this end, the Editors of this special volume of the *Review* invited seven scholars to consider watershed events and trends that have transformed educational research and practice, to reflect on what they have learned from research, teaching, and policy debates, and to offer thoughts about the future of research, policy, and the role of schools.

This collection deals with the intellectual history of educational research and assesses where it has come from, where it may be going, and where it must go. Though the authors cut into the subject from very different experiences and academic perspectives, they arrive at surprisingly related conclusions. The five broad papers discuss long-standing trends, but they are not optimistic, perhaps reflecting the current period of accumulating inequalities, polar-

Harvard Educational Review   Vol. 75   No. 1   Spring 2005

ized politics, international tension, and stasis or backward movement on some major dimensions of educational and social policy. They describe limited, partial efforts of mixed success, and none of the authors sketches any easy way to make progress in future efforts. In fact, I think that these pieces should make readers reflect on the complexity of the field of education. Though it has relatively low status in the academic world because of its attachment to low-paying and poorly respected and rewarded jobs, educational research has very demanding requirements and faces many obstacles. It is inherently interdisciplinary in nature; for example, no one could deny that educational development has psychological and sociological dimensions. Furthermore, few would contest that the interpretation and use of educational data and results are often highly political. This occurs within a society that assumes its schools can correct social wrongs and equalize opportunity. To understand the broad world of education research and policy, one must have a command of a variety of disciplines and techniques along with an understanding of the historical and legal grounding of the institutions and practices that affect schools and the external forces that shape educational opportunities. All education research takes place in a world where most of the major decisionmakers think that they know the answers without looking at any systemic data — they know it simply because they and their kids went to school.

The essays presented here critique the dominant issues in American education over the last seventy-five years — including testing, accountability, and markets — as severely inadequate ways to address the large problems in education. They are skeptical about the likely results of more scientific studies. After hearing the same things repeated by presidents and businessmen, think tanks and agencies, these writers are hungry for something deeper and more authentic, something that really gains purchase on our problems. Each of these articles contains serious warnings against the excessive narrowing of vision that comes with basing educational decisions on unexamined theories or test scores. The reductionism dictated by shrinking the value of a teacher or a school to a few decontextualized numbers disturbs the authors. The reification of those numbers into a definition of quality and value concerns them. From varied starting points, Ellen Condliffe Lagemann, Kieran Egan, Sonia Nieto, Jean Anyon, and Nelly Stromquist argue that our perspective must be far broader and we must not be trapped by fads, empty concepts, tautological arguments, or common wisdom taken as truth. Taking us beyond our own time and looking at both roots and possibilities are exactly what is needed now.

Ellen Condliffe Lagemann writes in support of educational research that would lead to scientifically valid, causal generalizations and increased use of experimental methods to find relationships that work independent of context. In this essay, however, she highlights the limits of that approach and the dangerous narrowing that would occur if those issues that can be addressed only through the humanities would be ruled out. Much of American education's intellectual development is, in fact, linked to studies of history and philosophy.

Turning to history, Lagemann narrates the development of the history of education field — including the attack by the history profession and the effort by education historians, under the leadership of Lawrence A. Cremin, to write more within the contemporary norms of the history profession. Yet, although this movement gained respect and status in the broader academic world, it turned out to be considerably less influential within American education than another movement that started not with disciplinary questions, but with the crisis of inequality in the schools and their failure to provide fair opportunities to all groups. According to Lagemann, the debates that came out of the critical analyses of inequality were more powerful because of their rootedness in serious current questions and interpretations that connected and captured imaginations. She says that it is essential to avoid an artificial attempt to turn all educational issues into scientific questions because "education is a form of human interaction that is full of uncertainties and therefore requires artfulness." She ends her essay by discussing the complexity and indeterminacy of important aspects of education and by advocating work that connects to real problems and does not despair if some of its most provocative and powerful insights come from other, more humanistic and intuitive ways of approaching explanation.

Kieran Egan's essay is a fascinating look at the rise of a master theory of children's intellectual development in American educational thought. As part of the Piagetian movement, Egan writes both from within it and from a longer historical perspective on why this theory became so profoundly influential and why it is not adequate as the basis for an evolving understanding. The confessional part of this piece includes a fascinating admission of the author's gradual loss of faith in the theories he had long taught, theories that "seemed to have very little hold on the everyday reality of schools and the great diversity among students." His students, many of whom were teachers, did not incorporate the theories in their work, and he worried about that. He describes the now largely forgotten but once overpowering influence Herbert Spencer's work had on theories of education in the late nineteenth century, which became the basis for many approaches to teaching and construction of curricula. Spencer's influence was based on his strong conviction that there was a knowable scientific method to teaching effectively. Much of this, however, was based much more on beliefs and assumptions than on any kind of scientific evidence.

More broadly, Egan finds that many of what seem to be basic theoretical principles turn out on close inspection to be a process of naming things and stating relationships that turn out to be tautological and in which "the principle is true simply because people define its terms to be something that cannot be other than true." The academic world and the world of policy often are most comfortable when there is a dominant theory that can frame work and investigations, but this essay strongly cautions us not to take dominance as proof of truth and never to lose sight of whether or not a theory is actually linked to reality and is useful to educators.

Sonia Nieto writes about the narrowing and betrayal of the promises of education in the recent past, particularly on issues of equity concerning race, gender, ethnicity, class, and language differences. To consider the broad trends of the past seventy-five years, Nieto chooses to focus on desegregation, bilingual education, and multicultural education, three major reforms of the past half-century. She notes how differing responses to the same conditions of the minority student achievement gap range from theories of genetic and cultural inferiority, to structures of social reproduction of embedded economic and racial inequality, to theories of incongruence of cultures between schools and the students they are now supposed to serve, to theories that some forms of school failure are actually political expressions of resistance to what the schools and society are trying to do. She offers a dazzling range of possible explanations and perspectives that would, of course, lead to differing kinds of school policies and interventions.

Nieto both discusses and reflects an ambivalence common among observers and students of U.S. schools, saying that "public education in the United States has been characterized by both extraordinary achievement and abysmal disappointments, and by everything in between. At the same time, it has remained the best hope for personal fulfillment and a more productive life for most segments of our population." Because of this, the schools are always a battleground for equality. To investigate this battleground, Nieto considers the desegregation struggle that began with intellectual work in the early twentieth century and was a central element of both the civil rights revolution of the 1960s and the conservative reaction that took hold in the 1980s. She further examines bilingual education, the nation's first serious response to the educational crisis of the Latino community, which involved respecting students' native language in a coherent transition into English fluency while retaining the native language as well. Nieto also considers multicultural education, another product of that civil rights reform. In the transition from physical desegregation to real integration, multicultural education provided curricula that included the history and culture of various groups of students and a recognition that their background should be respected in the schools.

Nieto concludes that the reversal of all of these policies shows the "widespread resistance to social change in U.S. public education" and notes that international comparisons find American schools "among the most unequal in the industrialized world." According to Nieto, education currently needs visionary researchers and writers with a broad understanding of American society and of how U.S. schools could better serve all children.

Jean Anyon's essay claims that educational improvement has lagged far beyond need and that no city during the last seventy-five years has ever been able to provide genuinely equal education for the poor. She concludes that social and economic structures dictate that politicians and schools almost always treat poor children and communities differently. But even beyond that, poverty hurts families and children in so many ways that poor children's education is almost inevitably doomed. Anyon concludes from this that economic and social policy are in fact educational policies, and that to create more equal schools on any scale we must address poverty, employment, income, and other basic social-policy issues. She believes that key elements of educational stratification must be addressed, but that if the substructure and the strong tendency of schools to reproduce the sector of society they serve are not dealt with, purely educational reforms will fail.

Educational research is often limited to things that happen in schools. But if a family does not have a secure place to live or if a parent is working full time at a minimum-wage job and her income is still below the level necessary to provide even the basic essentials of life, her children and their educational success are obviously going to be profoundly affected. In a society increasingly stratified by race and class, Anyon insists that educational researchers must seriously consider the possibility that educational outcomes cannot be understood or changed on any significant scale by research or policy interventions that do not change social and economic contexts, and the schools. In a society where schools are assumed to have great power, this is hard but good advice. We should never define the parameters of our thought or action by assumptions and should always be open to the idea that we may have to cross the boundaries of disciplines and policy arenas to actually improve educational opportunity.

Nelly Stromquist describes the intellectual developments since the Comparative and International Education Society was formed in 1969 as an interdisciplinary, international effort to reach general principles of knowledge about schooling. The initial premise of many in the field that education policy and institutions had strong transformative power, she concludes, gave way to "recognition that education is one force among many — one that is sometimes exploited politically to promise more than it can deliver." According to Stromquist, scholars have become less confident that theories will be developed that can explain educational outcomes across the world. The focus changed from an emphasis on explaining the interaction of parts of the system to a more critical view of inequalities and domination within the system and its relationship to those problems within societies. Work by scholars such as Paulo Freire has challenged the influence of quantitative research based on multivariate statistical models. Concern has increased regarding the differentiated and stratified models of education emerging in many countries as economic development occurs without a framework of social and economic equity. Increasingly, cultural, racial, and gender divisions are seen as fundamental problems for education. It seems clear that interpreting and changing the differentiated results of education requires an understanding of these issues. Stromquist sees strong evidence of the impact of external forces such as social movements, courts, social policy, and international agencies that help create a "contagion effort" of policy imitation. Looking at trends in the world's schools, she concludes that comparative educators must do more than observe and describe, but must respond to "growing global inequalities" with common action for policies favoring equal opportunity.

As an optimist who works on very hard issues of civil rights, I was puzzled when I first read these five papers by what seemed to be the emphasis not on accomplishments but on limits and the need for a change of perspective. Later the unifying and more hopeful elements became clearer. In this collection, there is a strong feeling that the present era is not one of great depth of understanding or sophistication, but a time of limits and disappointment in two intellectual projects that stemmed from the optimism of the early postwar-era explosion of empirical social science and the period of social and educational policy innovations and massive social change that came in the 1960s. In 2005, there is a feeling not only that that vision was naive in terms of overestimating the power of the schools and of our scientific tools, but also in underestimating the drag of complex and unequal societies. Too often what had been seen as progress was not. We didn't understand well the logic of the social sciences; we made false analogies and mistakenly transplanted them into concepts; we excluded vital parts that could not be quantified; and sometimes we got trapped thinking that tautologies were discoveries and that definitions were empirically grounded relationships.

So how do these authors suggest we improve educational research, policy, and practice? They ask us to expand our field of vision and to think seriously about social and economic structure, culture, and politics. They ask that our work be for something, that we be prepared to move beyond numbers and relationships, beyond inherited concepts and dispassionate curiosity, and that we think seriously about conditions that make educational equity virtually impossible. If the schools cannot function fairly because of these external forces and we know it, we must think seriously about our responsibilities to break open narrow and misleading discussions, to recognize that education without social policy will often fail, and, perhaps, to become active public citizens, following in the footsteps of Horace Mann, W. E. B. Du Bois, John Dewey, and other great leaders who combined analysis with commitment and action.

They call on us to avoid overly technical work as a sole solution, to engage with the great issues of the day, to admit when the emperor has no clothes, and to think seriously about not just the statistical relationships but the justification of systems that often mock the shared ideas of educational justice for all. All of these authors are committed to improving our schools. But they also call on us to come to this work with a healthy skepticism about simple answers, an appreciation of the historical and social context of schools, and the understanding that educational policy is only one part of a theory of change. They call for us to be more than researchers, more even than educators, not to violate the norms of science in what we claim to be fact, but also not to be afraid to talk more openly as citizens about experience, history, values, and politics.

I hope that this volume will generate a conversation that the *Harvard Educational Review* will carry on to the next stage, challenging readers and scholars to propose frameworks that respond to these suggestions and use them to produce questions and interpretations of data that will move us forward. Analysis and deconstruction are essential in the search for truth and good policy, but there is an equal need for imagination, commitment, and reconstruction of new visions and frameworks. I encourage the *Review* to start its next quarter century in that way. I encourage readers to consider their own responsibility to think about and react to these challenging interpretations and what they might mean for their own roles as citizens and leaders, and educators.

Does History Matter in Education Research? A Brief for the Humanities in an Age of Science

ELLEN CONDLIFFE LAGEMANN
Harvard Graduate School of Education

I am pleased that the Editors of the *Harvard Educational Review* have decided to devote their seventy-fifth anniversary volume to matters pertaining to education research. The topic is timely and important. It is timely because the state of education research has recently been a matter of considerable concern among scholars, policymakers, and philanthropists. Scholars inside and outside of schools of education have called for more rigorous and cumulative analyses of educational problems, while policymakers, frustrated with the seeming vagueness and irrelevance of many research findings, have lent their enthusiastic support to efforts to identify "what works" in education. In the meantime, many of the people who support education research have either abandoned the field or followed the drift of federal policy toward a preponderance of research that privileges large-scale, randomized experiments.

Personally and professionally I have favored many of the recent efforts to infuse a more scientific bent into scholarship about education. I tend to believe that studies of education have too often focused inordinate attention on the complexity of educational encounters and too little on the difficult problem of identifying factors that can be causatively related. I tend also to believe that policymakers are right to want answers — at least warranted probabilities concerning what will work, if not absolute certainties, regardless of culture and context. I also admire what can be learned from randomized trials, while worrying about their general feasibility and cost. Beyond that, while favoring more experimental work, I remain convinced that however valuable experimental and even quasi-experimental methods may be, we need an arsenal of varied methods and perspectives if we are to develop a rich and rigorously analytic understanding of education in all its forms.

Harvard Educational Review Vol. 75 No. 1 Spring 2005

Especially because I share some of the current worries about education research, I have often puzzled about what it is that has brought those worries to the forefront for so many of us interested in educational scholarship. One cause is certainly wide puzzlement concerning the seemingly intractable character of educational problems. Why do we spend so much money, work so hard, and appear to improve so little? Can we not do a better job of predicting whether and when a promising innovation will have promising results? Questions like these have driven some people to doubt the capacity of education research to inform practice and guide policy, and others to look for ways to enhance those relationships. Another possible cause for the current interest in the situation of education research must lie in the larger ecology of knowledge, for example, in the ever-increasing reliance on econometric styles of thinking across the social sciences. What is gained and what is lost as those styles gain more and more sway?

Even though it must be left to future generations of historians to eke out the multifaceted components of current curiosities, it seems safe to venture that there is at least one enduring element in present-day attention to the adequacy of education research. Because education matters so much, perfecting the ways we understand education is always urgent. The hope never seems to die (nor should it die) that better understanding will lead to more successful efforts to line up educational goals and instrumentalities. Armed with powerful research, it is hoped — and hoped repeatedly — that we will surely know what to do to achieve progress, prosperity, opportunity, equality, invention, and security through education. If, in the United States, education has always borne a large share of the perfectionist hopes that are so central to American culture, then cycles of concern about the state of education research must be understood as integral to those aspirations. If education is vital, so are the ways we study education. Just as education can never be good enough, so can methods for studying education never be sufficient to the challenge. It is because the work of people engaged in education scholarship is so urgent that it is always important to hold that work up to careful scrutiny. Are scholars asking the most significant questions? Are they posing those questions in the fullest possible contexts? Are they analyzing those questions with the most appropriate sets of methods, quantitative as well as qualitative, disciplinary as well as interdisciplinary? While it is timely within the context of contemporary education policy for the *Harvard Educational Review* to be recalling us to these questions, attention to them has enduring importance for all of us who study, practice, and care about education.

In what follows, I should like to focus on the history of the history of education as a way to query a central theme in recent discussions of education research. As I have indicated, many people, myself included, have argued that greater attention to the principles of science would strengthen the field of education research. Without in any way withdrawing my support for that call, I should like to suggest that in some instances efforts to develop more "scientific" forms of scholarship in education have not been beneficial. I think this is especially pertinent in those subfields of education scholarship that are aligned with the humanities, history, philosophy, literature, and the arts being central among them. In the past, questions about the value of history for the study of education have often encouraged historians to become more scientific. Today, amid new calls for science, this impulse should be resisted, I believe. Current calls for more science in the study of education should not be read — or misread — as insisting that all worthwhile scholarship in education must be scientific. Not at all — asserting that would not advance the field. Without the humanities, education research would be diminished. Humanistic and scientific perspectives must instead work in partnership, complementing one another with their differences.

The Origins of the History of Education in the United States

It would not be an exaggeration to say that the history of education scholarship in the United States began with the history and philosophy of education. At the end of the nineteenth century, when research universities were first establishing schools and departments of education, it was thought important to distinguish the university study of education from the study of education at normal schools. The claim was that normal schools were inferior because all they did was train teachers. By contrast, university-based schools and departments of education carried out the research that was meant to guide education policy and practice. To emphasize the more advanced character of the training they provided, pioneers like William H. Payne emphasized the importance of historical study.

To understand more recent debates about the value of history for educational study, it is useful to return to the nineteenth century and to look at least briefly at Payne's work. A little studied figure in the history of education, Payne taught at the University of Michigan with John Dewey before becoming chancellor of the University of Nashville (Vanderbilt today) and president of the Peabody Normal School. He believed that psychology, philosophy, and education should be linked to one another — an idea he passed on to the young John Dewey. Even though he thought psychology was just as important for education as anatomy was for medicine, he was also convinced that philosophy, which then encompassed history, was important. As the study of education became well established at research universities across the country, works such as J. K. F. Rosenkranz's *Die Pedagogik als System*, which was translated into English as *The Philosophy of Education* (1886), and two volumes by Gabriel Compayré entitled, in translation from the French, *Lectures on Pedagogy, Theoretical and Practical* (1887) and *The History of Pedagogy* (1885) became standard fare. So did Robert Herbert Quick's *Essays on Educational Reform* (1924) and major works by Plato, Rousseau, Pestalozzi, and Froebel (Lagemann, 2000).

Even though history was thus an early staple of educational scholarship, its value was called into question as the study of education became increasingly linked to the professional practice of education. That occurred first at Teachers College (TC) at Columbia University, which was by far the most important source of scholarship in education during the first half of the twentieth century. It was at TC that field after field of education research was defined — educational psychology, mathematics education, educational sociology, and, not least important here, educational history.

In 1897, TC's first great leader, Dean James Earl Russell, hired a man by the name of Paul Monroe, who had just finished his doctorate in sociology at the University of Chicago, then home to the nation's most outstanding sociologists. Russell urged Monroe to shift the focus of his work from the teaching of history to the history of education. Monroe's first publication, which appeared in 1901, was entitled *Source Book of the History of Education for the Greek and Roman Period.* Thereafter, he published a steady stream of similar volumes, including a *Text-Book in the History of Education* (1905). According to Monroe, the importance of that *Text-Book* lay in its avoidance of unsubstantiated generalization by resorting to "a body of historical facts" and the description of relationships between educational theories and actual educational practices, past and present. Monroe was suggesting that the *Text-Book* was a work of science — that is, that it was based on documentary evidence, or "facts," as opposed to opinions, suppositions, or untutored imagination. An increasingly popular ideal in American higher education at the time, science was becoming a more common source of scholarly authority. It was the claim that the *Text-Book* was a work of science that made it important.

Thanks to Monroe's efforts, the history of education, which had now become distinct from philosophy, became a major field of doctoral study at Teachers College. The famous early dissertations included: Henry Suzzallo's (1906) *The Rise of Local School Supervision in Massachusetts;* William Heard Kilpatrick's (1912) *The Dutch Schools of New Netherlands and Colonial New York;* Edgar Wallace Knight's (1913) *The Influence of Reconstruction on Education in the South;* and Robert Francis Seybolt's (1917) *Apprenticeship and Apprenticeship Education in Colonial New England and New York.* Even though works such as these created a literature for the field and even though some scholars deemed these works "scientific" because they were based on "facts," the history of education was not popular with master's students, who represented the largest segment of the student body at Teachers College. To them, the history of education lacked value because, however "scientific," it was not useful: It did not help them learn how to face the very real challenges of the classroom, and it was too detached from their professional concerns.

Bowing to this sentiment, scholars of the history of education began to narrow the field. In search of relevance, they began to focus on those historical forces that had directly shaped current professional problems and policies in education. Whereas Monroe's *Text-Book* had devoted only fourteen out of 761 pages to "The Present Eclectic Tendancy," most of the book having dealt with (unnamed) "Primitives, Orientals, Greeks, Romans, and Europeans," Ellwood Patterson Cubberley's (1919) *Public Education in the United States* began with a brief chapter on "Our European Background" and then devoted the rest of the book to "the battles" fought and won on the way to "new" (i.e., current) "fundamental principles" of education. Cubberley, who was the first dean of the School of Education at Stanford University, was determined in his quest to develop a "science" of education. Dismayed to discover that his colleagues in the arts and sciences did not think education should be considered either an art or a science, Cubberley nevertheless persisted in publishing works he considered scientific. His classic text in the history of education was but one example (Sears & Henderson, 1957, p. 70).

Narrowing to establish its relevance to practice-oriented students, the history of education became too professionalized — that is, too exclusively oriented toward the needs of would-be educators. It was no longer to be of interest to "real" historians — that is, to historians located in arts and sciences faculties. This latter group of historians provided the bulk of the membership of the professional associations in history. Not surprisingly, given their indifference to the history of education, neither the journal of the American Historical Association nor that of the Mississippi Valley Historical Association (now known as the Organization of American Historians) published a single article about the history of education during their initial decades in print. Still today, relatively few works on the history of education are reviewed in either of those journals. Most gain attention in the *History of Education Quarterly*, which is sponsored by the relatively small History of Education Society.

Even though its relevance was not evident to students and its general merits were not evident to professional historians, scholars of education continued to insist that the history of education was a necessary "foundation" for the study of their field. That rationale protected the history of education as a small but closely knit subfield of education research until the 1960s, when Bernard Bailyn and Lawrence A. Cremin led yet another effort to redefine it. They were responding to what Paul Monroe had earlier characterized as the "very general skepticism on the part of university faculties and of the departments of long standing, concerning the possibility of the scientific study of educational activities, either of exact, comparative, or historical character" (1910, p. 54).

Two Waves of Revision

Unlike Monroe early in the twentieth century, Bailyn and Cremin did not talk about "scientific history." To them it was "disciplinary" values that mattered, though the term now carried meaning not entirely different from the meaning of science in Monroe's day. If facts had distinguished scientific history for Monroe, more sophisticated matters of verisimilitude now distinguished disciplinary history for Bailyn and Cremin. If a reliance on facts had once been sufficient to suggest an effort to re-create the past as it had been (or as close as one living at a different time could get to that), now questions concerning purpose and context entered in.

Historians writing from a disciplinary perspective questioned whether professional purposes could be reconciled with scientific or disciplinary norms. This view became quite explicit during the late 1950s and early 1960s, especially within a group called the Committee on the Role of Education in American History, which was sponsored by the Ford Foundation's Fund for the Advancement of Education. Composed of historians and purposefully excluding historians who specialized in American education — put otherwise, purposefully excluding scholars who identified themselves as historians of education — the committee published a rather scathing review of the historiography of education. Characterizing the field as having had "a promising future and a disappointing present" for nearly a century, the committee recommended that the narrowing of the field so self-consciously undertaken by people like Ellwood Patterson Cubberley now be undone (Buck, 1957, p. 5). To write good history, the committee contended, education should be studied more broadly — not only in schools — and not in isolation from other historical forces, but rather as one among many forces shaping American society.

Three years after the Committee on the Role of Education in American History issued its report, Bernard Bailyn, a Harvard historian who had served as a member of the committee, published a slim "needs and opportunities" study about colonial education: *Education in the Forming of American Society* (1960). It had a stunning effect on the field and was frequently cited for years thereafter. Bailyn rightly insisted that most current literature in the history of education was anachronistic — insensitive to the meaning of things in their own time — because it was written with professional purposes in mind. This had resulted in the mistakenly narrow assumption that education was only what went on in schools. According to Bailyn, professional educators who had written the history of education to this point had forgotten that education was a much broader process than schooling. Rather than just schooling it was, in Bailyn's words, "the entire process by which a culture transmits itself across the generations" (1960, p. 14). Using a different measure of utility, a measure of the value of the history of education for history per se, a new generation of scholars was criticizing older generations who had used as their measure of value the relevance of the history of education to contemporary problems of education.

Bailyn's initial call for reform was loudly seconded by Lawrence A. Cremin of Teachers College in an essay entitled *The Wonderful World of Ellwood Patterson Cubberley* (1965). Cremin was the author of *The Transformation of the School* (1961), a prize-winning study of progressivism in education that, in fact, modeled the kind of historical writing the Committee on the Role of Education in American History and Bernard Bailyn had called for earlier. Cremin was unusual in that he was respected on both sides of the very wide 120th Street that separates Teachers College on the north from Columbia University on the south. Affiliated with but not officially part of Columbia, Teachers College was governed by a separate board, had its own budget, and maintained its own faculty. After publication of *The Transformation of the School*, Cremin was made a member of the Columbia University Department of History while maintaining his professorship at Teachers College, and came in many ways to embody the "new" field.[1]

In line with this redefinition, Cremin and a group of his colleagues at Teachers College remade the old TC Department of the Social and Philosophical Foundations of Education. Now known as the Department of Philosophy and the Social Sciences, "*The* Department," as its members proudly called it, was chaired by Cremin from 1958 to 1974, when he stepped down to become president of Teachers College. Appointments increasingly went to scholars trained in disciplines, who were known as professors of history (or philosophy, sociology, economics, or anthropology) *and* education, rather than as professors *of* the history of education.[2]

In addition to leading this well-publicized reform at Teachers College, an institution then still revered as a premier source of educational scholarship, Cremin won unprecedented support from the Carnegie Corporation of New York and the U.S. Office of Education to write a three-volume history, titled *American Education* (1970, 1980, 1988), that would model the newly broad and contextual approach. Although Cremin's trilogy was admired, it did not create a revolution in the field. I would even go so far as to venture that Cremin's efforts at Teachers College in creating the new Department of Philosophy and the Social Sciences may have been more widely emulated at other institutions, at least for a time, than Cremin's latitudinarian approach to the writing of history was emulated by other scholars.[3]

Cremin approached education via a definition that expanded over the years — education is "the deliberate, systematic, and sustained effort to transmit, evoke, or acquire knowledge, values, attitudes, skills, and sensibilities as well as any learning that results from that effort, direct or indirect, intended or unintended," he wrote in volume three (1988, p. x). The kind of broad cultural focus Cremin became known for did help stimulate some very exciting new literature about higher education, the intersection of religion and education, and politics and education. That said, I think it would be difficult to make a case that the reform Cremin led was as widely influential among scholars of the history of education as a second, subsequent reform initiated by Michael B. Katz.

Trained at the Harvard Graduate School of Education, Katz published *The Irony of Early School Reform* in 1968. In that work, he asked how a glorious, triumphant history of educational progress could be valid if the result was schools that were in crisis. As is the case again today, in the mid-1960s urban public schools were widely seen as failing poor children of color. This view was fueled by powerful exposés written by journalists like Jonathan Kozol and

Charles Silberman. Forcing scholars like Katz to question the apparent disconnect between past and present, the protest literature about public schooling encouraged not only Katz but also Joel Spring, who wrote from the perspective of an anarchist, Samuel Bowles and Herbert Gintis, who wrote from a Marxist perspective, and David B. Tyack, who wrote from a centrist perspective, to raise fundamentally new and challenging questions about the politics of education in the past and present. Now the motives of school reformers were called into question. Was it possible that elite school reformers had intended to use the public schools to socialize workers for life in factories? Was it possible that reformers had intended to introduce bureaucracy into once more informal school arrangements, thereby ensuring, for example, that better-paid men would supervise the largely female teaching force?

Triggering fascinating debate and making the history of education a topic of new interest both outside of and within schools of education, this second wave of revision became the subject of a review commissioned by the National Academy of Education and written by Diane Ravitch, then an adjunct assistant professor of history and education at Teachers College. It was presented to the academy in May 1976 and published by Basic Books in 1978. Called *The Revisionists Revised: A Critique of the Radical Attack on the Schools*, the Ravitch review savagely critiqued the questions raised, the sources cited, and the conclusion reached in most of the new revisionist work. Ravitch claimed that revisionist authors had confused outcomes and intentions and relied excessively on ideology to interpret evidence. Over and over again, she questioned the value of the sources they cited as well as the ways in which they had interpreted those sources. *The Revisionists Revised* had the effect of tamping down debate in the field. It did this for several reasons. First, because of its strident tone it was more widely read than a more measured review might have been. Additionally, because it came from the National Academy of Education, an honorific society in education that Cremin had helped to establish, many felt that Ravitch's piece seemed to be presenting an official line of the establishment among scholars of education. After publication of *The Revisionists Revised*, it was as if one had to declare whether one was "a radical revisionist," a term coined by Ravitch, or whether one was a follower of the more cultural reform effort. Proponents of "radical" revisionism were now presumed to be pitted against those favoring the earlier revisionist thrust associated with Bailyn and Cremin.

Subsequently, in 1985, political scientists Ira Katznelson and Margaret Weir published *Schooling for All: Class, Race, and the Decline of the Democratic Ideal*. Viewing history broadly, as Cremin had done, but approaching it with a neo-Marxist critical lens, Katznelson and Weir demonstrated that the Cremin and Katz waves of reform could, in fact, be joined with great benefit. Katznelson and Weir's scrutiny of the evidence led them to believe that many aspects of educational politics had not been inevitable, owing to economic relationships, but had resulted rather from the alliances and convergences of interest-group politics. This line of interpretation meshed with both Katz's sense that much about education history had had ironic outcomes and Cremin's belief that many education reforms had had both liberating and constraining outcomes. In consequence, Katznelson and Weir's work helped scholars recognize that, along with profound differences, there were points of overlap between the two schools of revision.

I should note at least one final point before I turn to some remarks about the value of history and other humanities for the study of education today, at the start of a new century. If I am right that the revisionist thrust led by Michael Katz had a greater influence on the questions historians asked and the frames they used than the revisionist thrust led by Lawrence Cremin, then it is important to understand why that is the case. I would venture that a significant part of the answer lies in the rootedness of Katz's work and that of others who advanced critical points of view in then-current questions of education policy and practice. It was the passion and the urgency of studying history to gain vantage on the present that made that stream of revisionism so lively and so important. It was the commitment to understanding history in order to change the present that gave the writings of the so-called radical revisionists power. By contrast, the Cremin latitudinarian approach seemed more "academic." Indeed, that is what it was meant to be — more responsive to developments within the discipline of American history.

What this suggests to me is that efforts to make history more academic, whether more scientific in Monroe's day or more disciplinary in Cremin's time, have tended to rob history of the contemporary social concerns that are necessary to enliven it and make it more than a string of dates, facts, and vignettes. This is because history must capture the imaginations of its readers to be of moment. It only becomes significant when it connects with enduring dilemmas or current puzzles and, in so doing, helps one see the present in more depth. Presentist concerns, in the sense I mean, are not professional concerns having to do with drawing exact lessons from the past to the present. They are not the kind of distortions everywhere in evidence in the writing of Ellwood Patterson Cubberley and others of his ilk. Presentist concerns, in the sense I mean, do not confuse the past as being a prior, lesser form of the present. Presentist concerns instead encourage one to understand the past on its own terms, as different from the present, and in drawing such a contrast help to illuminate both past and present.

That efforts to be scientific may tend to rob history of the presentist concerns that make it lively is more than a little ironic. After all, science is meant to be a vehicle for enhancing insight and advancing knowledge. While I certainly believe that science does enhance insight and advance knowledge and is very important for education, I would also contend that one must place limits on chasing science as a holy grail.

A Place for the Humanities in the New World of Educational Science

The cautionary tale I have tried to sketch here should have special value at the present moment in the history of education research. Even though it is too early to judge for certain, it would seem that the 2002 publication of the National Research Council (NRC) report, *Scientific Principles of Education Research,* represents something of a landmark in the history of educational scholarship. Setting aside claims that the study of education is unique in its complexity, the report asserted:

> At its core, scientific inquiry is the same in all fields. . . . [It] is a continual process of rigorous reasoning supported by dynamic interplay among methods, theories, and findings. It builds understandings in the form of models or theories that can be tested. Advances in scientific knowledge are achieved by the self-regulating norms of the scientific community, not, as sometimes believed, by the mechanistic application of a particular scientific method to a static set of questions. (Shavelson & Towne, 2002, p. 2)

Having served on the committee that wrote that report, I may well be biased. But I would venture that the report has ushered in a new day of interest in generating a rigorous science of education.

Whether that is indeed the case, it is clear that the NRC report has been mistakenly read as only supporting scientific approaches to education research. Beyond that, it has been mistakenly read as supporting large-scale randomized experiments, not only as the gold standard in education research but essentially as the only valid means for studying education. The report did *not* say that. The report is clear that, to understand education, a great variety of approaches is needed, including humanistic approaches such as history and philosophy. Regardless of what the report said, it is associated with the view that science, and science alone, must be the sine qua non of education research.

That is, of course, misleading. However difficult it may be to justify in this new age of science, the humanities have an indispensable role to play. Today, as I have suggested, the field of education research is focused on "what works" in education. The new Institute of Educational Sciences, which tellingly replaced the former Office of Education Research and Improvement in 2002, has provided significant funding for a new organization called the "What Works Clearinghouse." There, scholars are using meta-analysis to aggregate the findings of different studies of the effectiveness of different instructional interventions. The goal is to generate knowledge about which interventions are most effective.

Studies such as those underway within the "What Works Clearinghouse" are vitally important. We need tested knowledge in education. We need to know what works based on experimentation and empirical evidence. Education is too important to leave matters of instruction, assessment, school organization, and leadership to intuition and chance. That said, education is an enormously complex form of human interaction, and understanding it will require more than an understanding of techniques and how they work in different situations.

To understand education fully, we also need to appreciate its vagaries — the situations in which what was meant to work does not work, the situations in which unaccounted variations skew the weights of accounted-for variables. Education is a form of human interaction that is full of uncertainties, and therefore requires artfulness on the part of teachers and all who would foster learning. There are no certain ways to ensure that someone will have the kind of "ah ha!" moment when it feels like a light bulb has gone off in one's head. Such moments occur when one who has struggled to understand a connection suddenly goes beyond knowing that connection must exist to seeing it for one's self. Such moments occur when, in trying to master a new skill, one (seemingly) all of a sudden can do it, and do it again. If we could program such moments of enlightenment and mastery, which are often only recognizable after the fact, we would surely do so, but the likelihood of ever being able to do that, even as we develop a more rigorous science of education, is probably negligible.

Given the complex, uncertain character of education, it would be folly to believe that science alone can provide sufficient guidance to educational policy and practice. Science is the best way to illuminate laws, patterns, and regularities. It is not the best way to investigate human dilemmas, aberrant phenomena, or erratic occurrences. For those — for the unexpected, unwanted, unplanned events — the humanities are more powerful. The humanities — history, philosophy, literature, the arts, and aesthetics — expose us to what science cannot reveal. They open us to the buzz of a classroom, to the imponderable elements of exchange between teachers and students, each of whom ate (or did not eat) a different breakfast that morning and therefore came to school and came to that teacher's demonstration of electricity with a different readiness (or lack of readiness) to learn. The imponderable elements can be caught in a painting or a poem. They can be captured by retrospective accounts of life in a classroom. They can even perhaps be described by a theory of action, a philosophical statement. But they most assuredly cannot be captured by hypothesis-testing experiments. Were education scholarship to be robbed of the humanities — of history, philosophy, literature, the arts, and aesthetics of education — the field be greatly diminished. To allow calls for science in education to be read as calls not to advance the humanities in education would be a great mistake.

That the pendulum has swung so far toward science that we need to stand up and make the case for the humanities is worthy of note. It is worthy of note in the first instance because educators often resist the very idea of science in education. Scholars of education are more inclined to claim that each encounter is unique than they are to suggest that there may be patterns among educational encounters that should be investigated. They are more likely to focus on context and how differing contexts change educational encounters than they are to argue that there are commonalities that transcend context. Given that the default position for people who study education has usually been more oriented toward humanistic ways of knowing than toward the scientific, the current press for science is intriguing.

I suspect that this press arises, once again, from frustration with what are perceived to be failing schools. Lacking a sufficiently historical perspective, the public often forgets that commonly held goals in education have changed profoundly. Until publication of the famed Coleman Report — a study of equality of educational opportunity commissioned by the Office of Education in 1965, undertaken by sociologist James S. Coleman and published in 1966 — the goal for education in the United States had been to provide equal opportunities for education. Put otherwise, if a student had access to a classroom, that was deemed to be a sufficient fulfillment of public responsibility. After the Coleman Report, that changed. Thanks to this massive survey of the educational opportunities offered students in U.S. public schools that was intended to assess the merits of Title I of the Elementary and Secondary Education Act of 1965, public aspirations increased. Now, providing equal educational opportunities was no longer sufficient. Now, the goal was to provide equity — equal or near equal outcomes for all students regardless of race, class, religion, or ethnicity.

This very significant and totally appropriate shift in objectives slowly worked its way into the everyday expectations most Americans had for their public schools. It had become so much a part of the atmosphere by 1983, when the report of the National Commission on Excellence in Education appeared, that our schools were described as dangerously failing because they did not achieve equity. Entitled *A Nation at Risk*, that report was intentionally styled to present such a dire situation that it could not be ignored. "Our Nation is at risk," the report announced:

> Our once unchallenged preeminence in commerce, industry, science, and technological innovation is being overtaken by competitors throughout the world. . . . The educational foundations of our society are presently being eroded by a rising tide of mediocrity that threatens our very future as a Nation and a people. (quoted in Gordon, 2003, p. 167)

Since *A Nation at Risk* was published, the spotlight has remained on the nation's schools, the constant call being that they are failing and must be significantly overhauled — through more rigorous curricula, new governance systems (choice plans, vouchers, or for-profit education), and now, accountability, alignment of instruction and assessment, and instructional effectiveness. Only terrorist attacks and the Iraq War have moved education out of the number-one spot on the public agenda. This is unprecedented historically, education in the past having cycled on and off the stage after a decade or less of attention. The frustration that has built up after more than two decades of rightly faulting ourselves for failing to meet our educational objectives — our recently heightened educational objectives — has, I believe, fueled now-constant calls for educational science. Science is too often seen as a panacea and it is now expected to provide a panacea for one set of our toughest problems — our problems of educational policy and practice.

Assuming this analysis is correct and that frustration with school improvement has stimulated interest in educational science, then it seems especially important to counter this frustration and call for more science with an equally insistent effort to support work on the humanistic side of educational study. I favor more science in education. But I also worry that an overemphasis on science can result in an underemphasis on the humanities. Why, one might ask, has there not been more attention to the humanities in education? Why today do they seem to be so in peril, their value undermined by our rush toward developing "scientific principles for education"? I would suggest that if frustration with our failing schools has fueled our interest in developing scientific approaches to education, so, too, has what is called "the crisis in the humanities" fueled our tendency to overlook the importance of those perspectives.

The humanities have been in crisis for almost as long as I can remember. Chronically short of funds and challenged by more instrumental ways of knowing, the humanities are repeatedly justified by blue-ribbon commissions and proponents of liberal arts colleges. However, as the late historian Daniel Boorstin observed in his three-volume history *The Americans* (1958–1973), we are a practical people who revere know-how more than learnedness. We want to accomplish things more than we want to reflect. Boorstin would have found our newly preemptive foreign policy not the least bit surprising. It stems from a long-standing aspect of what he called the American character.

In light of this preference for instrumental knowledge, it is hardly surprising that the humanities should seem constantly to be under siege. Not as fully appreciated as their proponents would desire, the humanities have also been less well supported in education than those who believe in them think should have been the case. Intermittently, the federal government provides funds for science education through the National Science Foundation and other federal funding agencies. To my knowledge, there have never (or rarely) been federal funds available for the humanities in education. Only a few private foundations, notably the Spencer Foundation in Chicago, have supported scholars working in the history, philosophy, literature, arts, and aesthetics of education.

Via history, one can understand the imbalance currently so evident in calls for a science of education without an equal call for the humanities in education. Understanding must be a first step toward corrective action. Only if this imbalance is corrected will we be able to study education in a rounded and powerful way.

Reconciling Dualism

I like to think that John Dewey would agree with this position. I have long believed, as I have argued in print, that one cannot understand American education unless one realizes that Edward L. Thorndike won and John Dewey lost (Lagemann, 1989, 2000). Thorndike was the most famous psychologist Teachers College has ever had. He was a behaviorist and a vehement proponent of science in education, which was defined as the so-called laws of learning. Dewey, by contrast, was a connectionist who, following his Michigan colleague William H. Payne, tried to join psychology, philosophy, and education. Unlike Thorndike, Dewey was not an advocate of science defined as the laws of learning. Rather, he believed that science was anything that entered the hearts and minds of teachers and, by entering in, made them better able to teach and promote learning. Actually, Dewey spent many years and many volumes puzzling about science. And yet, even conceding some variation in usage, it is clear, I think, that he would not have supported current calls for a more rigorous science of education at the expense of the humanities.

Dewey wrote powerfully about the importance of art. The Laboratory School he led at the University of Chicago placed history, literature, and the arts at the center of the curriculum. He favored science, but did not believe it was a sufficient way to approach human experience. Dewey's lifelong quest as a philosopher was to reconcile dualisms. Springing from his deep interest in the writings of Hegel, this quest was even evident in many of the titles he (and, in some instances, his editors) gave to his best-known books, for example, *Democracy and Education* (1916), *Human Nature and Conduct* (1922), and *Experience and Nature* (1925). I tend to think, therefore, that Dewey would have favored more science in education so long as there was also more humanistic study. I hope he would have agreed that neither alone can be sufficient to offer us the understanding and guidance we need to provide more powerful education to more and more people.

In closing, I would like to return to the argument I laid out in the first part of this essay, the argument that history is most powerful when it embraces presentist perspectives rather than ones that are either more professional or more academic and scientific. I am aware that many people have argued that history is both a science and an art. It is a science because it is based on evidence — "the facts." It is an art because "the facts" do not speak for themselves. Their meaning must be imaginatively reconstructed and they must be interpreted, and to do that, one must imagine how one fact relates to another. While I accept the proposition that history is Janus-faced, I would still venture that history is most appealing and useful when its artistic or imaginative aspect is featured. It is this, after all, that enables one to see relations between past and present. It is this that makes history come alive.

Given the fact that science today is riding high and the humanities in education are underappreciated, it would be woefully easy for historians and other humanists to try to mold their studies in directions that appear scientific. To do that, I believe, would be a mistake. Rather, we must make the case for the humanities in education by demonstrating their utility. We must use the humanities in education to illuminate our dilemmas and uncertainties. We must use the humanities to understand the current — very important, if potentially overdone — call for science in education.

Notes

1. For additional information on Cremin see the biography that I wrote with Patricia Albjerg Graham, which is available at the Teachers College website: *www.TC.Columbia. edu/exhibits/cremin/lagemann-TCRecord.html.*
2. In the interest of full disclosure, I should point out that I was a Cremin student and that for almost twenty years I was a professor of history and education in the Department of Philosophy and the Social Sciences at Teachers College.
3. Again, in order to make clear where I stand in all of this, I should note that as a graduate student, I worked as a research assistant for Cremin as he wrote the second volume of *American Education.*

References

Bailyn, B. (1960). *Education in the forming of American society.* Chapel Hill: University of North Carolina Press.

Boorstin, D. J. (1958). *The Americans: The colonial experience.* New York: Vintage Books.

Boorstin, D. J. (1965). *The Americans: The national experience.* New York: Vintage Books.

Boorstin, D. J. (1973). *The Americans: The democratic experience.* New York: Random House.

Buck, P. B. (1957). *The role of education in American history.* New York: Fund for the Advancement of Education.

Compayré, G. (1885). *The history of pedagogy.* Boston: D. C. Heath.

Compayré, G. (1887). *Lectures on pedagogy, theoretical, and practical.* Boston: D. C. Heath.

Cremin, L. A. (1961). *The transformation of the school: Progressivism in American education, 1876-1957.* New York: Knopf.

Cremin, L. (1965). *The wonderful world of Ellwood Cubberley: An essay on the historiography of American education.* New York: Teachers College Press.

Cremin, L. A. (1970). *American education: The colonial experience, 1607–1783.* New York: Harper & Row.

Cremin, L. A. (1980). *American education: The national experience, 1783–1876.* New York: Harper & Row.

Cremin, L. A. (1988). *American education: The metropolitan experience, 1876–1980.* New York: Harper & Row.

Cubberley, E. P. (1919). *Public education in the United States.* Boston: Houghton Mifflin.

Dewey, J. (1916). *Democracy and education: An introduction to the philosophy of education.* New York: Macmillan.

Dewey, J. (1922). *Human nature and conduct.* New York: Henry Holt.

Dewey, J. (1925). *Experience and nature.* Chicago: Open Court.

Gordon, D. T. (Ed.). (2003). *A nation reformed? American education 20 years after A Nation at Risk.* Cambridge, MA: Harvard Education Press.

Katz, M. B. (1968). *The irony of early school reform: Educational innovation in mid-nineteenth century Massachusetts.* Cambridge, MA: Harvard University Press.

Katznelson, I., & Weir, M. (1985). *Schooling for all: Class, race, and the decline of the democratic ideal.* New York: Basic Books.

Kilpatrick, W. H. (1912). *The Dutch schools of New Netherlands and colonial New York*. New York: Teachers College.

Lagemann, E. C. (1989). The plural worlds of education research. *History of Education Quarterly, 29,* 185–214.

Lagemann, E. C. (2000). *An elusive science: The troubling history of education research*. Chicago: University of Chicago Press.

Monroe, P. (1901). *Source book of the history of education for the Greek and Roman period*. New York: Macmillan.

Monroe, P. (1905). *A text-book in the history of education*. New York: Macmillan.

Monroe, P. (1910). Opportunities and need for research work in the history of education. *Pedagogical Seminary, 17,* 54.

National Research Council. (2002). *Scientific research in education*. Washington, DC: National Academy Press.

Quick, R. H. (1924). *Essays on educational reformers*. New York: D. Appleton.

Ravitch, D. (1978). *The revisionists revised: A critique of the radical attack on the schools*. New York: Basic Books.

Rosenkranz, J. K. F. (1902). *The philosophy of education*. New York: D. Appleton.

Sears, J. B., & Henderson, A. D. (1957). *Cubberley of Stanford and his contribution to American education*. Stanford, CA: Stanford University Press.

Seybolt, R. F. (1917). *Apprenticeship and apprenticeship education in colonial New England and New York*. New York: Teachers College.

Shavelson, R. J., & Towne, L. (Eds.). (2002). *Scientific research in education*. Washington, DC: National Academy Press.

Suzzallo, H. (1906). *The rise of local school supervision in Massachusetts*. New York: Teachers College.

Students' Development in Theory and Practice: The Doubtful Role of Research

KIERAN EGAN
Simon Fraser University

A starting point for this examination of educational research during the past seventy-five years will be the reception, dismissal, hesitant acceptance, enthusiastic adoption, and apparent decline in the influence on education of Jean Piaget's ideas about development. Piaget's career conveniently spans the seventy-five year career of the *Harvard Educational Review*. However, his career is a conceptual rather than a sequential starting point for the topics to be discussed. The difficulties found in various theories of development in education form the focus for this article, and they exemplify some little considered but very serious problems for the ambition to bring scientific methods to the study of education. To put this topic into context, I briefly consider the main influences of developmental ideas prior to Piaget's work. This involves discussing the way Jean-Jacques Rousseau set in place the basic assumption on which development in education has been considered ever since, and the particular emphasis generated by the largely forgotten influence of the ideas of Herbert Spencer.

Perhaps Rousseau's, Spencer's, and Piaget's theories do not provide the best lens through which to view the contribution science was expected to make to education by those who most enthusiastically promoted a scientific approach to educational phenomena. Each theorist has always been somewhat suspect to the more self-consciously "scientific" researchers in education. But the move from one to the other and the increasingly pointed arguments about how to expose the nature of spontaneous development help me describe something of my own trajectory in responding to educational research during the past three decades or more. I came to North America just as the Piaget boom was getting underway, and I was an early enthusiast of his work. The way his theory worked from children's "illogical" answers was so refresh-

Harvard Educational Review Vol. 75 No. 1 Spring 2005

ing, and to me so brilliant. He also seemed to offer a much better understanding of the developmental process itself, and a better understanding of the educational interventions that would be congruent with children's spontaneous development.

I taught the introductory psychology of education course in my home university for a few years, and the more I taught Piaget's theory and its educational implications, the more I became skeptical about those claimed implications. In time I became increasingly skeptical about the theory itself, and then, running out of control, I became skeptical of most of the course content and especially of the claims made for the relevance to education of the psychological theories and research I was teaching. I think part of the problem was that so much of what I was teaching seemed to have very little grasp of the everyday reality of schools and the great diversity among students. As time went on, I began to wonder why so much research over such a long period of time did not seem to be having much purchase on education. Science surely ought to be able to do a better job of dealing with the phenomena of the field. It had worked wonders in other areas, so why was it so sluggish in dealing with education? I was familiar with many of the responses to this question, but came to be persuaded that the problem lay in something little commented on. I also began to wonder if many other educational researchers considered the question — "Has empirical research clearly benefited education?" — to be an *empirical* question. Despite grounds for some doubt about the general success of the enterprise, from general and depressing achievement data reported in such papers as the *New York Times* and the *Los Angeles Times*, and in works such as Ravitch and Finn (1987), it seemed an assumption that the answer would be positive. For so large an enterprise, there was little apparent attempt to address what surely should be one of the more energetically engaged questions.

Initially, like many researchers, I thought that the scale of research and research funding was paltry compared to the scale of the problems that we were expected to solve. I was also attracted to the view expressed by many researchers that the problem lay with teachers who were not attending adequately to all the knowledge that research was making available to them. But I began increasingly to recognize that many of the teachers in my classes were bright and committed people, and if this knowledge generated by research was having so little effect on their practice, maybe there were other explanations for its apparent irrelevance (apart from my incompetence as a teacher). I began to explore alternative explanations for the apparent failure of science to have much impact on education. I will describe briefly something of the path I followed with regard to developmental ideas.

Empirical or Ideological Bases for Change?

One of the puzzles I faced in exploring developmental theories was that I could not locate any obvious set of changes in educational practice that came in response to particular empirical results. The degree of influence of Piaget's theory on teaching methods and the curriculum, for example, seemed unrelated to empirical results of testing it. But let me approach the problem the way it came to bother me.

Early educational theories such as Plato's recognized that children's thinking is immature and that it becomes more sophisticated as children grow older. That increasing sophistication, however, was generally seen as a product of the social interactions in which children learned valuable knowledge from adults. Without more or less formal tuition, people remained intellectually childlike. In the common ancient Greek view, this was also the condition of adult "barbarians" (a Greek coinage derived from the way foreign speakers sounded to them: "bar bar bar bar"). That is, the minds of children were seen to have much in common with the minds of barbarians due to both groups not having received the formal instruction that would make their thinking more sophisticated. While there are suggestions in the premodern era of what today we generally take to be psychological development, such ideas were never clearly distinguished from the sense of development tied in with learning specific kinds of knowledge. For example, Plato — and, in fact, pretty well every other educational thinker before Rousseau — recognized that certain forms of theoretic abstractions became prominent in students' thinking in early adulthood. In the premodern world this was seen as something that happened to knowledge when the individual had accumulated a sufficient amount of it. The valuable knowledge that produced these desirable effects formed the core of an educational curriculum. It did not happen to the minds of those who had not learned that curriculum. This remains a plausible view, though it has largely been displaced by newer conceptions of psychological development.

Jean-Jacques Rousseau (1712–1778) offered an alternative view, whose radical nature we sometimes do not notice because we have come to take it completely for granted. In 1762 he published, in novel form — a rather odd novel, to be sure — *Émile ou de l'Éducation*. In this romance involving a boy reared apart from society, Rousseau introduced a set of revolutionary ideas that are a part of most modern educators' conception of education and that still guide much educational practice. Most significantly for present purposes, Rousseau suggested that the mind goes through its own distinctive developmental process, and the particular knowledge the student learns is only incidental to this development. Indeed, teaching the classical curriculum can interfere with the mind's spontaneous developmental process. He argued that the mind was a bit like the body; both go through regular stages of development, as long as they receive the appropriate environmental supports. For education, Rousseau argued, it was crucial to understand the spontaneous developmental process so that the teacher could conform to it and support it by providing the appropriate exercises, experiences, and knowledge. This is very much the dominant view today. It has led to what has been called a "biologized" view of the mind (Morss, 1990), for which it seems perfectly normal to use words like "growth" and to think of the mind as going through stages of spontaneous development. To those influenced by Rousseau, the mind ceased to be seen simply as an epistemological organ and came to be seen also, and to some exclusively, as a psychological organ. That is, instead of seeing the mind as made up of nothing other than the knowledge it has learned, people now see it as engaging in a range of psychological processes that are independent of the particular knowledge acquired.

In the premodern period, the kind of knowledge that was considered most valuable for building a sophisticated mind was summed up in the classical curriculum, in which Latin and Greek, philosophy, history, and theology formed the main pillars. The high status of this kind of knowledge was further undermined by the psychological approach embodied in the ideas of Herbert Spencer (1820–1903), who offered a distinctive shaping to ideas about psychological development. Most people in education today vaguely recognize Spencer's name, associating him perhaps with his curriculum-driving question, "What knowledge is of most worth?" This neglect of Spencer is perhaps understandable, given his association with the extreme social Darwinian ideas that went out of fashion toward the end of the nineteenth century, but is also astonishing, given his massive influence on education in North America. His book *Education: Intellectual, Moral, and Physical* was published in New York in 1860. By the end of the 1860s the book had been reprinted fifteen times by seven different publishers. Over the next few decades it sold hundreds of thousands of copies. It was the widest selling and possibly the most influential book on education published in North America during the period when U.S. public schools were being formed. Virtually everyone involved in education read it (Cremin, 1976; Egan, 2002).

Spencer influenced a number of modern conceptions of development. He became perhaps best known as an advocate of new evolutionary ideas. The problem was that his own conception of evolution was essentially Lamarckian. Jean-Baptiste de Lamarck (1744–1829) had proposed the first comprehensive theory of evolution in his *Philosophie zoologique* of 1809, in which he argued that changes occurred in species over time as acquired characteristics were passed on to their offspring. For example, if a species moved to a new environment in which stretching the neck was necessary to get food, the longer neck would be passed on to its children. Spencer was convinced that Lamarck's account of evolution was correct, and he never really understood the importance of Darwin's theory.

Spencer claimed to have brought to the concept of development what Rousseau had lacked — a scientific theory, derived from evolution. A related idea that Spencer contributed to educational thinking was the idea of progress. His Lamarckian view of evolution and his observation of the regularities that govern all the processes he studied led him to believe that "progress is not an accident, not a thing within human control, but a beneficent necessity"

(1851, p. 65). Spencer's essay on progress was among his most influential; it imbued many with a sense of great confidence that somehow the most fundamental processes of nature and society were providing a guarantee that we were moving gradually toward a more perfect world. Spencer tied ideas about evolution, development, and progress tightly together. The most powerful movement in education in North America, Progressivism, took its cue and its name from Spencer's central arguments.

Twentieth-century psychology inherited a conception of development that was intricately connected to a nineteenth-century conception of progress. Modern theories of cognitive development are most commonly "hierarchical integrative" — that is, each stage or phase of development contains, elaborates, and builds on the developments of the previous stage or stages. Consequently, each stage entails an addition without any sense that something might be lost in the process of "development" (Egan, 1997).

Spencer aimed to show how learning, development, and the daily activities of the classroom were subject to laws. The task for the scientific educator was to discover those laws and to let them shape educational practice for the benefit of children and teachers. Spencer's scientific agenda for educational research generated great optimism and set much of the agenda for educational research throughout the twentieth century. His own belief was that the progress he found in evolution was also evident in human history, and that children's development would recapitulate that progressive process. Spencer believed that he had found a scientific basis for recapitulation, unlike, say, Johann Friedrich Herbart (1776–1841), whose ideas about recapitulation Spencer considered based merely on imprecise intuition. He proposed recapitulation as a central principle for education. Spencer (1911) argued that the "education of the child must accord both in mode and arrangement with the education of mankind, considered historically" (p. 60). He believed that the child goes through, in a few years, the same process that took our ancestors millennia. By studying the process of mankind's historical progress one can discover principles for both methods of instruction and the curriculum. As with some of Spencer's other ideas, while many took up the underlying principle of a scientific approach to educational phenomena, the particular case of recapitulation ran into various forms of opposition. But the scientific approach to educational research was expected to "reveal pedagogic possibilities now undreamed of" (Hall, 1904, p. 222).

Spencer's ideas about development led to the formulation of some common instructional principles. In particular, Spencer promoted the idea that teachers should begin with the simple and move to the complex, begin with the concrete and move to the abstract, and begin with the known and move gradually to what is unknown. Spencer (1911) also claimed that "in education the process of self-development should be encouraged to the uttermost. Children should be led to make their own investigations, and to draw their own inferences. They should be *told* as little as possible, and induced to *discover* as much as possible" (p. 62). Superficially, some of these principles will seem familiar from the works of such people as Johann Heinrich Pestalozzi (1746–1827), Herbart, and Rousseau himself. And, certainly, these educators had considerable influence, especially Herbart, whose five steps for planning instruction were very widely used in America during the latter part of the nineteenth century and into the twentieth. What Spencer offered, however, was a coherent "scientific" account of education that was tied into a set of ideas that applied also to the physical and social worlds. It was the systematic vision that Spencer developed at encyclopedic length in a huge range of areas of inquiry that gave his work its compelling force, particularly in American education (Egan, 2002).

Education, Spencer wrote, had been most often conducted by forcing irrelevant information into the minds of reluctant children by methods that were patently barbarous. He proposed we should instead draw on new scientific principles to make the process efficient as well as pleasant for the child. In the past, education had dealt with subjects that held their place in the curriculum by dint of tradition and the pretensions to an ornamental culture of a leisured class; instead, he argued, we should make the curriculum of direct relevance and utility to the lives our students would actually lead. In the past, schooling was centered on the knowledge written in texts or authorized by teachers, whereas Spencer believed that the child's own developing needs and expanding activities should be central to the curriculum and to teachers' efforts. No doubt these ideas will appear familiar, even if they are not associated primarily with Herbert Spencer.

What is curious about some of these claims is the degree to which they follow assumptions derived from beliefs or ideology rather than research. The status of claims such as the notion that we should begin teaching with the known and gradually expand to the unknown, or with the simple and move to the complex, or the concrete to the abstract, will occupy us later.

Piaget's Reception

Piaget's long career, neatly framing the seventy-five years of this set of inquiries, began when he became a student of Pierre Janet in Paris. Janet had been strongly influenced by Spencer's ideas through the American, James Mark Baldwin. The influence of Spencer's "biologized" conception of development, his intricate connections between development and progress, and his assumptions of how one might go about establishing a scientific image of the developmental process are all clear in Piaget's work. Piaget's first books were translated into English about seventy-five years ago, including *Judgement and Reasoning of the Child,* which appeared in London in 1928, and *The Child's Conception of the World,* which appeared the following year in New York. While there was considerable scholarly interest in Piaget's work, it did not initially spur much in the way of curriculum development activities. Also, in a climate dominated by behaviorism, Piaget's unusual methodology and analyses of children's performance of odd tasks did not have a significant impact on mainstream thinking about development. Also, of course, the dominant theoretical issues of the day concerned the curriculum battles being waged between traditionalists and progressivists, and Piaget's ideas initially seemed to have nothing much to say to these.

By the 1950s, in Lawrence Cremin's words, "The more fundamental tenets of the progressives had become the conventional wisdom of American education" (1976, p. 19). While the language of education might have become progressivist, this did not mean that everyday practice had correspondingly changed. But the force of Cremin's observation apparently is not often recognized. The language of education in North America from the 1950s on became infused with progressivist assumptions. Even so, modern progressivist reformers think that education is dominated by an unmovable conservatism. The voices that receive the most enthusiastic response among educational researchers are those that promise to bring basic progressivist principles into practice. For example, if one were to look at the most influential modern voices in education, those that seem to bring us closer to realizing the progressivist promise for education are the most eagerly attended to: Eliot Eisner, Howard Gardner, Maxine Greene, and Nel Noddings all offer new insights into the meaning of the progressivist vision and how to bring it to realization. Those progressivist principles promised to make education more humane by adapting it to students' "natural" or spontaneous forms of learning and development. Progressive educators believed that scientific procedures could uncover what these processes were and devise compatible pedagogical methods.

Piaget's theory quickly gained an enormous audience when it was introduced in the context of Jerome Bruner's report of the Woods Hole conference, which was published in 1960 as *The Process of Education*, as supporting the progressivist aims of making education more humane, scientifically supported, and efficient. The older, "scientifically established" principles of education were considered a failure when the beeps of the Soviets' Sputnik were first heard around the world.

The trajectory of Piaget's reputation and the influence of his ideas on education have followed a curious route. During the 1960s his work became widely known among educational scholars, and its implications for education were explored. Among the many books that brought his work to the attention of American psychologists and educators during this period one might note John Flavell (1963), Hans Furth (1970), David Elkind's studies and his book of 1976, and Richard Ripple and Verne Rockcastle's edited book of 1964, along, of course, with a steady flood of books from Piaget and his collaborator, Barbel Inhelder. Piaget's name began to appear in curriculum documents in many states in the late 1960s and 1970s, often accompanied by a note that his ideas about children's development deserve some attention. In the 1970s and early 1980s, his developmental theory began to have a serious impact on curriculum revisions around North America and Europe, and his name was commonly found in such documents with more or less elaborate sketches of his "stages of development." By the late 1980s, his name appeared less and less in such documents, while his often unattributed theory was represented simply as how children developed. What was at first represented as a theory that might be of some interest had almost entirely lost its status as a theory. Piaget had become almost invisible in such documents, but his ideas remained fundamental to the definition of child development and its implications for practice (Roldão, 1992). Since the 1990s, Piaget's general reputation has suffered from increasingly compelling criticisms, yet his theory's influence on curriculum documents and teacher-education texts marches on. For example, *Time* magazine notes, "Although not an educational reformer, he championed a way of thinking about children that provided the foundation for today's education-reform movements" (Papert, 1999, p. 104). Also, it seems fair, still, to accept Susan Sugarman's 1987 judgment that "despite appearances to the contrary, Piaget's ideas and overall approach continue to dominate much of developmental psychology" (p. 241), and even more so, developmental ideas in education.

If one were to look at research on Piaget's theory in education, one would not find that the rise of his reputation coincided with sets of positive empirical tests of the theory from the 1960s to the 1980s. On the one hand, researchers consistently replicated Piaget's classic conservation experiments, though there were irregularities in results and much argument about the criteria for what counted as conservation, for example. But in general, Piaget's genius in attending closely to the peculiar answers children gave to his questions led to a genuine revolution in theorizing about their intellectual development. For millennia people had been hearing the odd logic of early childhood and had usually dismissed it as a kind of intellectual froth to be blown away by more mature forms of thinking. Piaget made it a cornerstone of his theories. As a scientific theory, however, Piaget's frameworks rested on a set of experiments that remained somewhat contentious. In many of the experiments, for example, instructions were given orally, and many found it difficult to conclude whether what the experiments were disclosing was a common sequence of language development or the development of underlying operative structures, as Piaget claimed. Despite such doubts about Piaget's methodology, no competing theory provided more insights into intellectual development. On the other hand, the enthusiasm for Piaget's work was much stronger in education than even in psychology. Projects and programs in curriculum and instructional methods were underway across the continent. Much of this educational work was uninformed by reliable research that showed comparisons between Piagetian programs and others. What research there was suffered the usual problem: The programs that were to be compared were not simply different means to an agreed and common end; the methodological difference also reflected different educational objectives. It had gradually become clearer during the seventy-five years we are looking at that in education, following a physical science model of comparing alternative treatments just did not deliver the kind of results expected. Progressivist methods, for example, might well be found to be less "efficient" in achieving particular results, compared with forms of "programmed learning." But, progressivists pointed out, the acquisition and memorization of particular knowledge was not the only educational aim. As Dewey had pointed out, in education the aim is tied up in the method used; one uses progressivist methods because they are a part of what you are trying to achieve educationally, not simply because they are the most efficient method of ensuring memorization of some knowledge.

Even so, some large-scale research projects were attempted, comparing programs whose teachers had been trained in Piagetian methods with the results of regular schools teaching the same curriculum. Charles Brainerd reviewed four large comparative studies and concluded that the evaluation data, which included children's performance on concrete-operational content and a range of fairly standard Piagetian activities and also standardized achievement tests (see Brainerd, 1978), "have failed to show any differences between Piagetian instruction and other curricula" (p. 298). Indeed, in one of the Piagetian schools that was compared with a traditional school, Brainerd concluded that "those few comparisons which revealed differences tended to favor the traditional group" (1978, p. 293).

A theory that promised to show how a scientific approach to development could revolutionize pedagogy ought to show better results. Piagetian writings for teachers commonly made strong claims about the results that would follow if teachers attended to the theory and shaped their instruction and curricula accordingly. Such knowledge of the process of development would have, in a continuing echo of G. Stanley Hall (1904), "pedagogical possibilities now undreamed of" (vol. 2, p. 222). The odd feature, of course, is that the inconclusive results of Piagetian research seem to have had little impact on the enthusiastic reception of Piaget's ideas in education.

Empirical Science and Conceptual Analysis in Studying Education

A background hum to these explorations — a bit like the background radiation from the Big Bang — was Ludwig Wittgenstein's brief but rather pointed observations about the state of psychology. Wittgenstein's claim follows from the recognition that there is no such identifiable thing as "the scientific method." Science proceeds by working out sets of questions that can be addressed to particular kinds of phenomena to result in certain kinds of answers. Phenomena, questions, and acceptable answers are intricately tied together. The problem with psychology, Wittgenstein said, was that "the existence of the experimental method makes us think we have the means of solving the problems which trouble us; though problem and method pass one another by" (1963, p. 232).

If that was the background hum, an observation more in the foreground about scientific research in education was the guidance offered by its theories. The main source of my growing skepticism about Piaget's theory, and then about many others I had been teaching, was tied up with another of Wittgenstein's observations about psychology. He characterized the psychology of his day as suffering from a defect that might also be directed at much current educational research: He saw a combination of "experimental methods and *conceptual confusion*" (1963, p. 232; emphasis in original).

Lev Vygotsky (1997) made an argument similar to Wittgenstein's, which also helped me understand why so much of the work that was based on psychological theories seemed to have so little purchase on educational phenomena:

> A concept that is used deliberately, not blindly, in the science for which it was created, where it originated, developed and was carried to its ultimate expression, is *blind*, leads nowhere, when transposed to another science. Such blind transpositions, of the biogenetic principle, the experimental and mathematical method from the natural sciences, created the appearance of science in psychology which in reality concealed a total impotence in the face of studied facts. (p. 280)

While that may seem an overwrought judgment about psychology in general, it captured what was bothering me about psychology's contributions to basic educational concepts, such as "learning" and "development."

Take the conclusions that Spencer derived from his developmental theory, that learning and teaching should move from the simple to the complex, the concrete to the abstract, the known to the unknown. Are these ideas supported by scientific research? They are taken for granted by nearly everyone in education as far as I can tell, but how did they get that status?

What bothered me most about Piaget's theory was not the methodological issues, but rather the fact that educators seemed to use his progress-dominated theory to support principles similar to those that Spencer had articulated. For example, Piaget's theory was used to support practices based on the principle that the teacher should move from the "concrete" to the "abstract." This is a principle that came to be embodied in the social studies curriculum, beginning with the local, empirical environment and moving gradually to more distant, conceptually grasped environments — stimulated, again, by Spencer — and it has led to the insistence on beginning with "hands-on" activities and manipulation of objects prior to conceptualization about them. However, given the definition of those two terms in Piagetian theory, in which later stages incorporate the achievements of the earlier ones, how could the abstract have preceded the concrete? That is, in some degree the sequence seemed not a matter for empirical verification; it is true by definition of the terms (Phillips & Kelly, 1975). Similarly, Piaget also implied that the developmental direction from the simple to the complex and from the known to the unknown was supported by empirical research based on a scientific theory.

Consider the ubiquitous principle that one must move from the known to the unknown: "If I had to reduce all of educational psychology to just one principle, I would say this: The most important single factor influencing learning is what the learner already knows. Ascertain this and teach him accordingly" (Ausubel, 1968, p. 235). There is something conceptually confusing about such claims resulting from psychological research.

First, if this is a fundamental principle of human learning, there is no way the process can begin. That is, the principle sets one into an infinite regress looking for prior learnings. Now obviously that is not what the researcher or teacher uses the principle for, but if the principle is to make sense we need to be able to discover some starting point for the process. That we cannot do this in any sensible way should alert us that something is wrong with the principle.

Second, if novelty — that is, things unconnected with what is already known — is the problem for human learners, reducing the amount of the novelty does not solve the problem. And if we can manage some novelty, why can we not manage more? That is, the principle tells us to tie new learning to old learning because, it implies, students cannot grasp things that are unconnected with what they already know. But if they are to learn *anything* new, which they do all the time, this shows that students can learn things that are, in some degree, however small, unconnected with what they already know. So why insist on a principle whose sole justification is based on something obviously false? (We'll see below why people hold to the principle despite such gaping flaws.)

The third objection is less directed at the principle than at how it has been invariably interpreted in education, and particularly in the construction of the elementary social studies curriculum. Many educators assume that what children know first and best is the details of their everyday social lives. That is, they assume that children's thinking is simple, concrete, and engaged with their local experience. But children also have imaginations and emotions, and these, too, connect with the world. If children's minds are supposed to be restricted to the everyday details of their social lives, why are they full of monsters, talking middle-class animals like Peter Rabbit, and titanic emotions? Elsewhere I (Egan, 1997) have commented on the absurdity of explaining Peter Rabbit's appeal in terms of its "familiar family setting," when it involves a safe woodland and a dangerous cultivated garden, and death so close, and so on.

Fourth, and this is perhaps a doubtful notion to suggest, a few moments' reflection should make clear that no one's understanding of the world expanded and expands according to this principle of gradual content association. The neat process of gradually "expanding horizons" might appeal to the curriculum developer concerned that prerequisite knowledge is constantly in place to ensure a smooth progress through the math or science curricula, but if you reflect on how your understanding of the world and human experience has grown, and continues to grow, you will likely find that it is a much messier and more unpredictable and wild process.

One might similarly analyze the three other principles and show that they too are very dubious. What is "concrete" about children's learning language early on? Perhaps learning the meaning of "table" might be, oddly, called concrete, but how can learning the meaning of "and" and "but" be concrete in any sense? What "concrete" instruction is required for the child to master such terms? These principles seem to have an odd status, in that they seem almost true by definition, but at the same time they seem full of holes the more closely one analyzes them. I concluded, aided by Jan Smedslund (1978a, 1978b, 1979), that the reason such doubtful principles retained their force in education was due to their being, like most knowledge claims in education — or so it increasingly seemed to me — a mixture of analytic truth and empirical generalization. That is, at some level the principle is true simply because people define its terms to mean something that cannot be other than true. So, in the case of the "known to unknown" principle, it is understood to mean something like, you do not know whatever you do not know and if you learn something new, it has to fit in with what you can find comprehensible. Put like this, the principle is just a logical truth — you do not have to run an experiment to discover that a person cannot understand something they lack prerequisite knowledge for. At this level, the principle is not very helpful. What would make it interesting are reliable empirical generalizations; that is, research showing conditions that constrain learning that are other than logical truths. We largely lack these in education because researchers commonly mix up analytic elements — things that are true by definition or by logic — with empirical components — things that could be otherwise but are discovered to be true as a result of experiments. By consistently mixing the two, we get claims that are assumed to be empirical generalizations resulting from research but whose generalizability relies heavily on the analytic component hidden in how the principle is formulated.

Smedslund analyzed various pieces of social science research and showed that they were mostly what he called pseudo-empirical; they claimed to have established empirical connections when their positive findings actually relied on prior conceptual connections. A. R. Louch (1966) had shown earlier how much research in psychology had similar defects. He began with the example of Edward Thorndike's "law of effect," which claimed to have established that people choose to repeat behaviors that have pleasurable consequences. Louch pointed out that the connection between repeating behaviors and expecting pleasurable consequences is not conceptually independent. The two behaviors are analytically tied: What we mean by choosing to repeat behaviors is tied up with what we count as pleasurable consequences. Louch further noted that E. R. Hilgard's list of findings firmly established by psychological research were similar in kind. Hilgard's (1956) first proposition was that "brighter people can learn things less bright ones cannot learn" (p. 486). But what we *mean* by brightness involves the ability to learn more. Or take a more recent example. In the *How People Learn* project the aim has been to focus on findings that "have both a solid research base to support them and strong implications for how we teach" (Donovan, Bransford, & Pellegrino, 1999, p. 12). The basic principles derived from carefully applying these criteria include the finding that: "To develop competence in an area of inquiry, students must (a) have a deep foundation of factual knowledge; (b) understand facts and ideas in the context of a conceptual framework; and (c) organize knowledge in ways that facilitate retrieval and application" (p. 12). Such claims seem to have a similar character to those above. Clearly a, b, and c are definitional of what we *mean* by competence in an area of inquiry. Empirical research could not have established that one could be competent in an area of inquiry without deep factual knowledge (and how deep is "deep"?), or without understanding facts and ideas in the context of a conceptual framework, or while organizing knowledge in ways that hindered retrieval and application. It may prove of practical value to spell out the meaning of competence like this, but the spelling out could have been done without the empirical research that is supposed to have established these conditions of competence.

Let me try to expose the problem with these kinds of research "findings" by giving a simple example. Let us imagine a team of researchers exploring how students learn and memorize information. They might run an experiment that involves the students in learning randomly ordered seven-digit numbers. If one student's randomly assigned number is her telephone number, the results of the experiment would be contaminated by this arbitrary coincidence. But a sufficiently large sample will neutralize the irregular result in this case.

Let us further assume that this experiment with learning random seven-digit numbers is part of a study that is testing the hypothesis that ordered information is more easily memorized and remembered than random or disordered information. An educational implication of supporting the hypothesis, it might be claimed, is that it will help us understand how to present information to students, particularly if we have to organize it in list form. After the experiment, and many others like it conducted with different populations, the researchers might feel confident in claiming that their research has shown that ordered lists are learned more easily than random lists.

But this would be another pseudo-empirical finding. The analytic component concerns the conceptual ties between order and learnability. Our mind's ability to learn and our notions of what counts as ordered are connected before and regardless of whatever research shows about their relationship. If students in the experimental group learned random lists more easily than ordered lists, the researchers would have scanned the lists for some order they had failed to notice earlier. On discovering that, in one case, the supposedly random number was the student's telephone number, they would feel satisfied that they had accounted for the anomalous result. What we *mean* by order is conceptually connected to what we can more readily recognize and learn. No experiment is required to establish the generalization.

In the experimental group, however, there will have been some variability among subjects' learning and memorizing the random numbers. The telephone coincidence is just one dramatic anomaly, but then there will be the case of the numbers that are, for another student, his mother's birth date, and the one that is only a digit different from another student's bank account code, and so on. Certainly not all random numbers will look equally random to all subjects, but these findings are arbitrary. Researchers control for them by having large samples and other methods. What they cannot do, of course, is generalize from these anomalies. Researchers cannot generalize about that student's ability to learn and memorize random numbers or about other students' ability to learn and memorize those particular numbers.

So in the case of this research there is an analytic tie that guarantees a strong positive correlation both between orderedness in the lists and the ease of learning and memorizing and between randomness and difficulty. There is, in addition, a range of arbitrary elements that will have ensured that what counts as ordered for one subject will seem random to another, and a variety of indeterminable arbitrary contaminants in the data. By confusing the two, by failing to distinguish the analytic component from the arbitrary components, researchers will likely treat the results of the study as an empirically established connection. The analytic component, however, generalizes absolutely. The arbitrary elements cannot be generalized at all. Establishing the analytic component does not need an experiment. And the arbitrary elements, which are genuinely empirical, cannot be generalized.

Conclusion

Rousseau's and Spencer's biological model of human development generated a range of assumptions, which continue to influence how teachers are prepared and how children are expected to learn. Although Rousseau's biologized conception of the mind helped to refute the old notion of a metaphysical and mystical mind distinct from the body, his modeling of the development of the mind on that of the body was excessive. It is far from clear, for example, that food's contribution to our bodily development is very like knowledge's contribution to our minds' development. In the latter case, knowledge becomes a constituent of the mind in a way that food does not become a constituent of the body — eating lots of spinach will not make you look more like a spinach, but the mind *is* shaped by the kinds of experience and knowledge it takes in. Spencer's idea of progressive development and learning gave us those ubiquitous practical principles of moving from the known to the unknown, from the simple to the complex, from the concrete to the abstract. Piaget's more elaborated account of the developmental process supported both progressive educational ideas and Spencer's principles. Despite the important contributions of these thinkers, they have left us with some deep dilemmas about the role and value of empirical research in education.

The usual way of representing education's relationship with scientific psychological research is to suggest an analogy — physics : engineering :: psychology : education. The increasingly preferred version seems to be biology : medicine :: psychology : education. But psychology is not a science like physics or biology. And education is unlike engineering and medicine: It is value saturated in the way engineering is only marginally, and both medicine and engineering do not have radically different goals asserted for their activities in the way that is common in education. Asserting the analogy seems to replace presenting an argument, as though the analogy were pellucid rather than obfuscating.

It is still the case that anything claimed in education without the support of empirical research is dismissed as speculative, or, as the summary of the *How People Learn* project puts it, what is now "subject to powerful research tools" was in the past "a matter for philosophical arguments" (Donovan, Bransford, & Pellegrino, 1999, p. 5). The implication is that cognitive science will now clear up what was formerly mere speculation or philosophical arguments, just as the physical sciences cleared up and displaced speculation and philosophical arguments about, say, the nature of the objects visible in the night sky, the causes of diseases, and so on. It is increasingly unclear to me that this is an accurate way of seeing the relationship between psychology and education. The assertiveness of cognitive scientists in laying a claim on "science" seems misplaced. Basic conceptual work has been avoided and left undone, and we go ahead with precisely the kinds of confusion that Wittgenstein pointed out some years ago. Methodological sophistication cannot compensate for a lack of conceptual clarity; method and problem pass one another by.

The waning of Piaget's theory has been accompanied by more attention to Vygotsky's ideas. Some of the interesting areas being opened up follow on Vygotsky's ideas about how students pick up cognitive tools as they grow up in a society, and also about his ideas on the development of imagination. This has facilitated research of a primarily analytic kind into the sets of cognitive tools that come along with an oral language, such as stories, metaphor, forming images from words, and so on, and then working out how one can design frameworks for planning teaching that build in these tools. One can similarly analyze the sets of cognitive tools that come along with literacy, such as fascination with the extremes and exotic, association with heroes, engagement by wonder, and so on, and work out how these too can facilitate imaginatively engaging learning. Such an approach leads to quite distinctive conceptions of development, focusing on the kinds of understanding we can construct with our "cognitive tool kits," and also to new and potent methods of teaching that focus on engaging the imagination. (One source for this work is available at http://www.ierg.net; also see Vygotsky, 1997, 2004.)

Oddly enough, this newer Vygotskian program takes us closer to Plato than to the kinds of conceptions of development that have held sway in education from Rousseau's time through the years of Piagetian dominance. A concern with "cognitive tools" drives us more in the direction of epistemological constructs than anything like Piagetian operations. A concern with stimulating and developing cognitive tools takes one immediately to analysis of the curriculum content that constitutes the tools in question; that is, from seeing the "cultural tools" that can become "cognitive tools" for each child. The continuing dominance of progressivist thinking in North America has led, during the recent period of increasing Vygotskian influence, to slightly bizarre attempts to suggest that Piagetian and Vygotskian theories are coherent or compatible, despite attempts to show how inappropriate such conflations are (Kozulin, Gindis, Ageyev, & Miller, 2003; Wertsch 1985, 1991). It is as though — to use Piagetian language — Vygotsky can be accommodated in North America only if he is assimilated to progressivist assumptions. It is of course presumptuous of me to suggest, at a time when progressivist tenets remain almost at the level of presuppositions in educational thinking, that psychological developmental theories of the kind that have dominated educational thinking on the topic are an aberration and they are finally beginning to lose their hold. The lack of any clear empirical demonstration of their benefit to education must, in the end, lead toward their dissolution. In their place, we may hope to see attempts to generate *educational* theories of development, whose character will be more sensitive to the phenomena of education than to those of psychology and which will likely gain sustenance from Plato and Vygotsky rather than Spencer and Piaget. The problem is to find ways to characterize the successive modes in which children make sense of the world and of their experience in a language that leads us directly to distinctive curriculum content and new methods of teaching. (An attempt to frame such a theory may be found, I am only moderately ashamed to point out, in Egan, 1997.)

References

Ausubel, D. P. (1968). *Educational psychology: A cognitive view.* London: Holt, Reinehart and Winston.

Brainerd, C. J. (1978). *Piaget's theory of intelligence.* Englewood Cliffs, NJ: Prentice-Hall.

Bruner, J. (1960). *The process of education.* Cambridge, MA: Harvard University Press.

Cremin, L. A. (1961). *The transformation of the school.* New York: Vintage Books.

Cremin, L. A. (1976). *Public education.* New York: Basic Books

Donovan, S., Bransford, J. D., & Pellegrino, J. W. (Eds.). (1999). *How people learn: Bridging research and practice.* Washington, DC: National Academy Press.

Egan, K. (1997). *The educated mind: How cognitive tools shape our understanding.* Chicago: University of Chicago Press.

Egan, K. (2002). *Getting it wrong from the beginning: Our progressivist inheritance from Herbert Spencer, John Dewey, and Jean Piaget.* New Haven, CT: Yale University Press.

Elkind, D. (1976). *Child development and education: A Piagetian perspective.* New York: Oxford University Press.

Flavell, J. H. (1963). *The developmental psychology of Jean Piaget*. Princeton, NJ: D. Van Nostrand.

Furth, H. G. (1970). *Piaget for teachers*. Englewood Cliffs, NJ: Prentice-Hall.

Hall, G. S. (1904). *Adolescence: Its psychology and its relations to physiology, anthropology, sociology, sex, crime, religion, and education* (vol. 2). New York: D. Appleton.

Hilgard, E. R. (1956). *Theories of learning*. New York: Appleton-Century-Crofts.

Kozulin, A., Gindis, B., Ageyev, V. S., & Miller, S. M. (Eds.). (2003). *Vygotsky's educational theory in context*. Cambridge, Eng.: Cambridge University Press.

Louch, A. R. (1966). *Explanation and human action*. Berkeley: University of California Press.

Morss, J. R. (1990). *The biologizing of childhood: Developmental psychology and the Darwinian myth*. Hove, Eng.: Lawrence Erlbaum Associates.

Papert, S. (1999, March 29). Jean Piaget. *Time*, pp. 104–106. Available online at http://www.time.com/time/time100/scientist/profile/piaget.html.

Phillips, D. C., & Kelly, M. E. (1975). Hierarchical theories of development in education and psychology. *Harvard Educational Review, 45*, 351–375.

Piaget, J. (1928). *Judgement and reasoning of the child*. London: Routledge and Kegan Paul.

Piaget, J. (1929). *The child's conception of the world*. New York: Harcourt Brace Jovanovich.

Ravitch, D., & Finn, C. E., Jr. (1987). *What do our 17-year-olds know? A report on the first national assessment of history and literature*. New York: Harper & Row.

Ripple, R. E., & Rockcastle, V. N. (1964). *Piaget rediscovered*. Ithaca, NY: Cornell University Press.

Roldão, M. do C. (1992). *The concept of concrete thinking in curriculum for early education: A critical examination*. Unpublished doctoral dissertation, Simon Fraser University, Burnaby, British Columbia.

Smedslund, J. (1978a). Bandura's theory of self-efficacy: A set of common-sense theorums. *Scandinavian Journal of Psychology, 18*, 1–14.

Smedslund, J. (1978b). Some psychological theories are not empirical: Reply to Bandura. *Scandinavian Journal of Psychology, 19*, 235–252.

Smedslund, J. (1979). Between the analytic and the arbitrary: A case study of psychological research. *Scandinavian Journal of Psychology, 20*, 101–102.

Spencer, H. (1851). *Social statics*. London: Chapman.

Spencer, H. (1928). *Essays of education and kindred subjects*. London: J. M. Dent. (Original work published 1911)

Sugarman, S. (1987). *Piaget's construction of the child's reality*. Cambridge, Eng.: Cambridge University Press.

Vygotsky, L. S. (1997). *The collected works of L. S. Vygotsky* (vol. 3; R. W. Rieber & J. Wollock, Eds.). New York: Plenum.

Vygotsky, L. S. (2004) Imagination and creativity in childhood. *Journal of Russian and East European Psychology, 42*, 7–91.

Wertsch, J. V. (1985). *Vygotsky and the social foundation of mind*. Cambridge, MA: Harvard University Press.

Wertsch, J. V. (1991). *Voices in the mind: A sociocultural approach to mediated action*. Cambridge, MA: Harvard University Press.

Wittgenstein, L. (1963). *Philosophical investigations* (G. E. M. Anscombe, Trans.). Oxford, Eng.: Blackwell.

Public Education in the Twentieth Century and Beyond: High Hopes, Broken Promises, and an Uncertain Future

SONIA NIETO
University of Massachusetts Amherst

Public education and democracy have been firmly linked in the popular imagination since at least 1848, when Horace Mann, in his twelfth annual report to the Massachusetts State Board of Education, declared, "Education then, beyond all other devices of human origin, is a great equalizer of the conditions of men" (1868, p. 669). Half a century later, and just a few short years before the *Harvard Educational Review* published its inaugural issue, John Dewey's (1916) progressive notions about education cemented the link between education and democracy. According to Dewey, schools could serve not only to level the playing field, but also as an apprenticeship for civic life. Current proclamations about public education seem strangely at odds with these sentiments. Now the talk is more about testing and rubrics than about democracy and equality, making it clear that we have strayed far afield from the ideals articulated by Mann and Dewey.

In commemorating the *Harvard Educational Review*'s 75th anniversary, it is useful to reflect on how and why the goals of public education have seemingly shifted in such a dramatic way. In this article, I argue that the quintessential questions of public schooling over the past seventy-five years, and the answers to them, have emerged primarily from the changing demographics in our nation and schools. That is, changes in population in terms of race, ethnicity, social class, and other differences have helped to shape the educational experience of all students in our schools. I also suggest that the history of the past seventy-five years will influence how, as a nation, we view, design, and implement public education in the coming century.

Harvard Educational Review Vol. 75 No. 1 Spring 2005

In what follows, I present a broad overview of the hopes and disappointments of K–12 public education over the past seventy-five years, as well as the prospects for its future. Differences in race, ethnicity, social class, language, gender, sexual orientation, religion, and exceptionality, among others, have all defined inequality in public education. Each of these issues has also been the subject of important struggles for educational equality throughout the past century. One brief essay, however, cannot hope to address all these concerns fairly. Therefore, I have chosen to focus on race, ethnicity, social class, and language, and have selected as case studies three major efforts to equalize learning for all students that have responded to these four concerns and that have subsequently shifted the historical development of our public schools. These three efforts — desegregation, bilingual education, and multicultural education — will also no doubt influence future directions for school reform.

I begin with the changing nature of the student population and how it has affected the opportunities offered by public schools, and whether those opportunities have brought us any closer to public education as the democratic "equalizer." As part of this discussion, I review a number of theories advanced over the past century to explain the underachievement of students of diverse cultural, linguistic, and racial backgrounds. I then present brief case studies of the social and educational movements that responded to inequality as it has been manifested in various ways and in different communities: desegregation, bilingual education, and multicultural education. How these efforts have been thwarted is the subject of the next section, and I conclude with reflections on the need to renew the nation's commitment to public education and the public good in the coming century.

Changing Demographics, Changing Classrooms

Although the United States has always been a multiracial and multiethnic nation, it is far more diverse today than it was seventy-five years ago when the *Harvard Educational Review* was inaugurated. As of the year 2000, people of color made up 25 percent of our total population, a 5 percent increase from just a decade earlier. This growing racial and ethnic diversity has been accompanied by a growing linguistic diversity: Currently, 18 percent of U.S. residents speak a language other than English at home, with Spanish the language spoken by half of these (U.S. Census Bureau, 2000a). Also in 2000, the number of foreign-born or first-generation U.S. residents reached the highest level in U.S. history, 56 million, or triple the number in 1970. Unlike previous immigrants who were primarily from Europe, only 15 percent of recent immigrants come from Europe, with over half from Latin America and a quarter from Asia (U.S. Census Bureau, 2002).

It should come as no surprise, then, that the nation's public schools are also very different from what they were just a few decades ago. Although not yet a majority, the number of children in our public schools who represent backgrounds other than European American is growing rapidly: Whites still make up more than half of all students, but they are a dwindling majority, at just 61.2 percent. Blacks comprise 17.2 percent, Hispanics, 16.3 percent, Asian/Pacific Islanders, 4.1 percent, and American Indian/Alaska Natives, 1.2 percent of students in public schools (National Center for Education Statistics, 2002).

Besides differences in race/ethnicity and language, our nation is also characterized by growing disparities in wealth, and it is especially bleak among people of color: while Whites represent just over 9 percent of the poor, Blacks are over 22 percent and Hispanics over 21 percent of those living in poverty (U.S. Census Bureau, 2000b).

Theories of Achievement: Changing Contexts, Changing Explanations

Given the changing demographics of students in U.S. schools, the discrepancy in academic achievement among various groups of students has been the subject of much speculation and research for several decades. Since almost the beginning of the twentieth century, competing theories have been advanced to explain what is now known as the "minority achievement gap," that is, the difference between the academic achievement of White, middle-class students and their peers of other social and cultural backgrounds, especially African Americans, Latinos, and Native Americans, as well as some Asian Pacific Americans. These theories have positioned students in various ways: as genetically inferior, culturally deprived, culturally different, economically disadvantaged, victims of structural inequality, and more. Because explanations of academic failure and success have been at the center of much educational policy and practice in K–12 education over the past century, I briefly review some of the more salient theories below.

Genetic and Cultural Inferiority

One of the most popular theories throughout the past several decades has been that students of racial minority and economically poor backgrounds are genetically or culturally inferior. This theory, which gained great momentum in the 1960s, was made by such researchers as Frank Reissman (1962), Carl Bereiter and Siegfried Engelmann (1966), and, most persuasively, by Arthur Jensen in a controversial but nevertheless influential 1969 *Harvard Educational Review* article, in which he posited that the poor achievement of African American students could be explained mostly by genetic differences. Although the terms used then (*culturally deprived, genetically inferior*) may be out of favor now, these viewpoints held great sway during the 1960s, and they were responsible for much of the social and educational policy made in the following decades. The assumption behind these theories was that students' failure to achieve

45

could be explained by their so-called deficits, including their genetic makeup, poorly developed language skills, and inadequate mothering, among others.

William Ryan, an early critic of deficit theories, helped lay the groundwork to challenge such theories by arguing that they represented a strategy to "blame the victim." He wrote:

> We are dealing, it would seem, not so much with culturally deprived children as with culturally depriving schools. And the task to be accomplished is not to revise, amend, and repair deficient children, but to alter and transform the atmosphere and operations of the schools to which we commit these children. (1972, p. 61)

Ryan's eloquent argument against deficit theories notwithstanding, genetic and cultural inferiority theories are not a thing of the past. They survive, albeit couched in different terms. Current discourse continues to position marginalized groups as predetermined low achievers by using buzzwords such as "at risk" and "disadvantaged," terms reminiscent of the reasoning used as the basis of the theories made popular in the 1960s. In addition, such terms are based on a psychological framework that lays the blame primarily on students' individual and cultural characteristics rather than on structural inequality, social class inequality, and racism. This reasoning, in turn, supports questionable policies and practices that further jeopardize students of nonmajority backgrounds. For example, Catherine Banks (2004) points out that the imprecise and widely used label "at risk" became a funding category for state and federal educational agencies, making the terminology popular with bureaucrats and thus perpetuating a particular way for teachers and administrators to think about such students. Viewing at-risk students and their families as being primarily responsible for student failure to learn has meant that more deepseated issues of inequality and injustice have often been neglected.

Economic and Social Reproduction Theories

Beginning in the 1970s, activists, educators, and researchers challenged deficit theories by insisting that structural inequality, racism, and poverty — issues overlooked by deficit theories — could better explain students' poor academic achievement. Revisionist historians and economists such as Joel Spring (1972) and Samuel Bowles and Herbert Gintis (1976) suggested that schools tend to serve the interests of the dominant classes by reproducing the economic and social relations of society. Michael Katz (1975), for instance, demonstrated that from the start, public schools were "universal, tax-supported, free, compulsory, bureaucratically arranged, class-biased, and racist" (p. 106). According to Katz, these seemingly contradictory features derived from the very purpose of public schools, which was largely to train different segments of society for particular roles in life. As a result, these historians and economists claimed, schools reproduced the status quo and not only reflected structural inequalities based on class, race, and gender, but also helped to *create and maintain* these inequalities.

Economic and social reproduction theorists maintained that the "sorting" function of schools, to use a term coined by Spring (1972), is apparent in everything from physical structure to curriculum and instruction. For example, the schools of the poor are generally factorylike fortresses that operate with an abundance of bells and other controlling mechanisms, whereas the schools of the wealthy tend to be much more open physically and psychologically, thus giving students more autonomy and opportunities for creative thinking (Anyon, 1981). Moreover, relations between students and teachers in poor communities reflect a much more dominant-dominated relationship than in middle-class or wealthy communities (McDermott, 1977). Hence, the sorting function of the schools replicates the stratification of society. The benign, stated purpose of U.S. schools as an "equalizer" was seriously questioned by these theories.

The arguments of the social reproduction theorists have had a tremendous impact on educational thinking since the 1970s. But by concentrating primarily on the labor-market purpose of schooling, they tended to fall into a static and mechanistic explanation of school success or failure. Put in its most simplistic form, this analysis assumes that schooling is simply imposed from above and accepted from below. Yet because schools are complex and perplexing institutions, things are not always as neat or apparent as the theory of social and economic reproduction would suggest. The lengthy struggles over schooling in which many communities have been historically engaged — including desegregation, bilingual education, multicultural education, and access to education for females and students with special needs — are not accounted for in these theories. Some theorists, such as Michael Apple (1986), have suggested instead that schools are a product of conflicts among competing group interests, and that the purposes of the dominant class are never perfectly reflected in the schools, but rather are resisted and modified by the recipients of schooling.

Cultural Incompatibility Theory

Another explanation for school failure, the cultural mismatch or cultural difference theory, emerged in the early 1970s as a counterpoint to the cultural deprivation theory. According to this theory, because school culture and home culture are often at odds, the result is a "cultural clash" that gets in the way of student learning. As a result, the differing experiences, values, skills, expectations, and lifestyles with which children enter school, and whether these differences are consistent or not with the school environment, need to be considered. The more congruent home and school cultures are, the reasoning goes, the more successful students will be. Some of the theorists who promoted this line of thinking also identified institutional racism as being at the core of cultural mismatches. For example, the link between cultural mismatch and racism was eloquently articulated in an earlier *Harvard Educational Review* article by Baratz and Baratz (1970).

Cultural mismatch theories have continued to evolve, albeit with various names and subtle differences (cultural compatibility, cultural congruence, cultural competence, cultural responsiveness, culturally relevant and culturally appropriate instruction, among others). In the early 1980s, for example, Katherine Au (1980) was instrumental in identifying what she called *cultural congruence in instruction* as an important consideration in educating Hawaiian children. Gloria Ladson-Billings (1994), in coining the term *culturally relevant teaching*, has suggested that this kind of pedagogy is in sharp contrast to *assimilationist teaching*, whose main purpose is to transmit the dominant culture's beliefs and values in an uncritical way to all students. In the same vein, Geneva Gay's (2000) work in defining and explicating what she calls *culturally responsive teaching* has been significant.

The cultural mismatch theory has been a more hopeful explanation for school achievement than explanations based on genetic inferiority or economic reproduction because it assumes that teachers can learn to create environments in which all students can be successful learners. Hence, it respects teachers as creative intellectuals rather than simply as technicians.

Sociocultural Explanations for School Achievement

Another closely related theory links the cultural practices of particular communities with their students' learning in school settings. Shirley Brice Heath's (1983) classic research with a Black community that she called "Trackton" is a persuasive example of the power of aligning teaching to students' cultural practices. She found that the kinds of questioning rituals in which the parents and other adults engaged with children were not preparing the children adequately for school activities.

Middle-class parents, for example, usually speak Standard English, and they also tend to engage in school-like prereading activities much more regularly than do working-class parents. Also, in observing the White, middle-class teachers of these children, Heath found that the questions they asked students were qualitatively different from the kinds of questions the children were accustomed to at home. Teachers' questions concerned pulling attributes of things out of context and naming them (e.g., to identify size, shape, or color). In contrast, in their homes the children were asked questions about whole events or objects, as well as about their uses, causes, and effects. These questions, which were frequently linguistically complex and required children to have a sophisticated use of language, also required them to make analogical comparisons and understand complex metaphors. Usually there was no one "right" answer, because answers involved telling a story or describing a situation. The result of the different kinds of questions asked in the different contexts was a perplexing lack of communication between students and teachers.

Heath's work, although similar to notions of cultural incompatibility, was based primarily on differences in language practices that were made clear through ethnographic research. For example, through a research project with

Heath, the teachers became aware of the differences in questioning rituals, and they began to study the kinds of questions that adults in Trackton asked. Teachers were then able to use these kinds of questions as a basis for asking more traditional "school" questions, to which children also needed to become accustomed if they were to be successful in school. The results were dramatic: Children became active and enthusiastic participants in these lessons, a notable change from their previous passive behavior. Heath's landmark research has been followed by many other studies based on sociocultural theories that explain student learning (e.g., Willis, Lintz, & Mehan, 2004).

Students as Castelike Minorities

In an alternative explanation of school failure and success, in the 1970s anthropologist John Ogbu (1987) began developing a highly influential theory that goes beyond cultural discontinuities. He suggested that in order to understand academic outcomes it is necessary to look not only at a group's cultural background, but also at its situation in the host society and its perceptions of opportunities available in that society. Ogbu classified most European immigrants in the United States as voluntary immigrants, and racial minority group immigrants as either voluntary or involuntary minorities, that is, those who come of their own free will as opposed to those who were conquered or colonized. According to Ogbu, involuntary minorities are those who have been incorporated into the United States against their will and thus have a "caste-like" status in the society. These include American Indians, African Americans, Mexicans, and Puerto Ricans.

Ogbu concluded that voluntary minorities tend to do better in school than those born in the United States because their self-esteem and school success depend not just on their ethnicity, but also on their interaction with U.S. society. Moreover, they tend to arrive in the United States with strong self-concepts developed in their home countries, where they are not seen as minorities. On the other hand, according to Ogbu, most voluntary minorities have a "folk theory" of school success that sees the United States as a land of opportunity, where one gets ahead through education and hard work.

According to Ogbu, given the long history of discrimination and racism in the schools, involuntary minority children and their families are often distrustful of the education system. It is not unusual for students from these groups to engage in what Ogbu called *cultural inversion*, that is, to resist acquiring and demonstrating the culture and cognitive styles identified with the dominant group. These behaviors, considered "White" by such students, include being studious and hardworking, speaking Standard English, listening to European classical music, going to museums, and getting good grades. Instead, involuntary minority students may choose to engage in what Ogbu called *oppositional behavior*, emphasizing cultural behaviors that differentiate them from the majority and are in opposition to it. These students must cope, in the words of Signithia Fordham and John Ogbu, "with the burden of acting

White" (1986, p. 186). They see little benefit from academic success, at least in terms of peer relationships. Those who excel in school may feel both internal ambivalence and external pressures not to manifest behaviors and attitudes that would define them as academically successful.

John Ogbu's theories have been helpful in explaining the differences in the school experiences of students of various backgrounds. But they have also come under criticism for being incomplete, ahistorical, inflexible regarding individual differences, and rigid in defining immigrants as either voluntary or involuntary. Ogbu's theories may place an inordinate responsibility on students and families for improving academic performance without taking into account either institutional racism or what Claude Steele (2004) has called the *stereotype threat*, that is, how societal stereotypes about particular groups can influence their academic performance. In addition, his explanation of oppositional culture comes dangerously close to the old concept of the culture of poverty popularized in the 1960s.

Resistance Theory

Resistance theory, as articulated by scholars such as Henry Giroux (1983), Jim Cummins (1996), Herb Kohl (1994), and others, adds another layer to the explanation of school failure. According to this theory, *not* learning what schools teach can be interpreted as a form of political resistance. Frederick Erickson (1993) maintains that whereas cultural differences may cause some initial school failures and misunderstandings, it is only when they become entrenched over time that a consistent pattern of refusing to learn arises.

Resistance theory is helpful because it attempts to explain the complex relationship of disempowered communities with their schools. Students and their families are not only victims of the education system, but also actors in it. They learn to react to schools in ways that make perfect sense, given the reality of the schools, although some of these coping strategies may in the long run be self-defeating and counterproductive.

An extreme form of refusing education is dropping out. Michelle Fine's (1991) landmark ethnography of a large urban school found that most dropouts were actually stronger students than those who stayed in school. The dropouts she interviewed expressed two major reasons for their decisions to leave school: a political stance of resistance, and disappointment with the promise of education. Many were articulate in their resistance to school, and even some of those who stayed were unsure what benefits they would derive from their education.

Care, Student Achievement, and Social Capital

An issue that has received great attention since the early 1990s in explaining student success or failure is what Nel Noddings (1992) has called the "ethic of care." For her, care is just as — and in some cases, even more — important than entrenched structural conditions that influence student learning. In this theory, whether and how teachers and schools care for students can make an immense difference in how students experience schooling. However, care does not just mean giving students hugs or pats on the back. It also means loving them by having high expectations and making rigorous demands. Angela Valenzuela (1999), in a three-year exploration of academic achievement among Mexican and Mexican American students in a Texas high school, provides compelling examples of how care among a small number of teachers made a difference in students' engagement with schooling. This was the case in spite of the general context of the school that provided what Valenzuela called *subtractive schooling*, that is, a process that divested students of the social and cultural resources they brought to their education, making them vulnerable for academic failure. Her research led Valenzuela to locate the problem of underachievement not in students' identities or parents' economic situation, but in school-based relationships and organizational structures. Similarly, Nilda Flores-González (2002), in a study of Latino students in Chicago, came to the conclusion that school structures and climate help create either "school kids" — that is, those who connect with schooling and thus have a better chance to succeed — or "street kids" — those who have largely given up on school because they do not see it as a place where they belong.

Another theory closely connected with the ethic of caring is described by Ricardo Stanton-Salazar (1997) as a social capital networks framework. According to Stanton-Salazar, social networks reproduce or deny privilege and power, and they are of key importance between adults and youth, particularly vulnerable youth who rarely have access to the social capital that more privileged students take for granted. The networks and institutional supports he identifies include particular discourses and social capital; access to gatekeepers and to other opportunities usually closed to disenfranchised students; advocacy; role modeling; emotional and moral support; and advice and guidance. In the end, Stanton-Salazar argues, it is through the power of institutional agents such as teachers, counselors, and other adults who can manipulate the social and institutional conditions in and out of school that can determine who "makes it" and who does not. The support provided by these institutional agents is linked with caring because it is only through trusting and close relationships with teachers that students will gain access to such networks.

Newer Perspectives

This brief review of some of the many theories of school achievement to describe the experiences of students of diverse backgrounds makes it clear that there is no simple explanation for student success or failure. Many of the theories developed over the past century have been inadequate or incomplete: some have failed to consider the significance of culture in learning; others have not taken into account the social, cultural, and political context of

51

schooling; still others have placed all the responsibility for academic failure or success solely on students and their families.

Newer perspectives concerning the education of new and old immigrant groups of color in the United States have emerged in the past several years, and they add significantly to our understanding. For example, Alejandro Portes and Rubén Rumbaut (2001), in a series of long-term, comprehensive studies of immigrant families of various backgrounds, concluded that the process of growing up as an immigrant in the United States ranges from smooth acceptance to traumatic confrontation. They found that race is a paramount factor in whether and how groups are accepted into the mainstream, and it can trump the influence of other factors such as social class, religion, or language. They found, for example, that immigrants fleeing from Communism are received more favorably than those fleeing economic exploitation. They cite Haitians, Nicaraguans, and Mexicans as economic refugees, who have significantly lower earnings than Cubans and Vietnamese, even after controlling for level of education, knowledge of English, and occupation. No matter how long they have been here or how hard they work, the earnings of Mexicans, Nicaraguans, and Haitians remain consistently low, while those of Vietnamese and Cubans, viewed as political refugees, increase for each additional year of residence in the United States. Portes and Rumbaut (2001) come to the startling conclusion that no matter how educated a Mexican or Haitian is, his or her chances of moving ahead economically are significantly constrained by the social environment in which their group has been incorporated into the United States. For these groups, a college degree yields no improvement in earnings. This conclusion flies in the face of conventional wisdom that education equals economic advancement. Clearly, other factors — race, context of incorporation, and others — are also at work.

High Hopes

The above discussion leads to the inevitable conclusion that school achievement, always difficult to explain, must be approached by taking into account multiple, competing, and dynamic conditions: the school's tendency to replicate society and its inequities; cultural and language incompatibilities; the unfair and bureaucratic structures of schools; the nature of the relationships among students, teachers, and the communities they serve; and the political relationship of particular groups to society and the schools. Given the complexity of the problem, it is not surprising that public education in the United States has been characterized by both extraordinary achievement and abysmal disappointments, and by everything in between. At the same time, public education has remained the best hope for personal fulfillment and a more productive life for most segments of our population. In fact, public schools have been the major battleground for many movements to extend civil rights and privileges, not only those having to do directly with education.

Expanding Equal Educational Opportunity

Since free public education first took hold in the late nineteenth century, expanding educational opportunities to benefit a greater number of children has been of paramount importance for many educators and citizens. With increasing racial, linguistic, and economic diversity in our nation and schools, the challenge to expand the dream of an equal education for more students has been even greater. In fact, calls for equal education have riveted the nation's attention during much of the twentieth century, whether through the civil rights movement led by African Americans and their allies, or other movements that resulted in school boycotts and takeovers, or court challenges and commission hearings. In what follows, I offer a brief review of some examples of these struggles, focusing on desegregation, bilingual education, and multicultural education.

— Desegregation

The history of desegregation represents the greatest manifestation of the struggle for equal education in the twentieth century. African Americans in the South were especially victimized by the Jim Crow doctrine of "separate but equal" schools, a doctrine that made a sham of the promise of equal education. Black schools, always inferior to White schools in terms of infrastructure and resources, nevertheless often provided nurturing and academically supportive environments for African American children (Siddle Walker, 1996). But racially segregated schools were also evident in other parts of the country. Gloria Ladson-Billings (2004), for instance, has documented the long history of African Americans' attempts to desegregate public schools, beginning as early as 1849 in Boston. Until recently, segregation was firmly etched in the popular consciousness as being only a Black/White issue. Yet other groups also experienced segregated schooling. A number of historians, including leading scholars and activists such as W. E. B. Du Bois (2001), George Sánchez (1940), and Carter Woodson (1933), began unearthing the multiracial history of segregation based on race and ethnicity many years ago. Besides African Americans, Mexicans and Native Americans were especially negatively affected by segregation. Other groups denied an equal education, through either outright exclusion or segregation, included Chinese and Japanese children, primarily in California but in other states as well (Pang, Kiang, & Pak, 2004).

Dismantling de jure segregation did not happen overnight, of course. Although segregated schools were a fixture in many places around the country, it was not until the momentous 1954 *Brown v. Board of Education* decision that segregation by race in public schools was finally declared illegal. The *Brown* decision, universally recognized as the case that shot down the doctrine of "separate but equal," is also considered by some to be the most pivotal event since the Fifteenth Amendment of 1870, which granted all male Americans the right to vote (Ramsey & Williams, 2003).

Since the 1970s a new generation of historians has taken on the task of documenting the multiracial history of unequal education (Anderson, 1988; Donato, 1997; Ruiz, 2001; San Miguel, 2001; Spring, 2004; Tyack, 1995; Weinberg, 1977). The brutal history of boarding schools in the Native American community, for instance, has only recently been brought to light (Archuleta, Child, & Lomawaima, 2000; McBeth, 1983). Mexican Americans, the Latino group with the most extensive experience in the United States, also faced a long history of exclusion. Yet few people, even educators, recognize the less well known but also watershed moments of their struggle for equal education in such cases as *Independent School District v. Salvatierra* in Texas (1930), protesting the segregation of Mexican children; *Roberto Alvarez v. Lemon Grove* in California in 1931 (see Alvarez, 1986), the first successful desegregation case in U.S. history; and *Méndez v. Westminster* in California's Orange County (1945), which ended the segregation of Mexican children in California schools. Some of these cases, in fact, served as legal precedent for the *Brown* decision. More recent immigrants, including Central Americans and Asian Pacific Americans, have also faced unequal schooling and have engaged in numerous activities from legal challenges to demands for school reform to change the situation (Rumbaut & Portes, 2001; Suárez-Orozco & Suárez-Orozco, 2001).

The struggles for equity in the past seventy-five years that emerged from the civil rights movement provide a graphic illustration of the hope and promise that U.S. public schools hold, particularly for those communities that have been marginalized in our society. Yet it is a sad fact that segregation in public schools is on the rise today. The continuing struggle for desegregation and equal access highlights the certainty of challenges in the future.

— Bilingual Education

In the United States, language use and patriotic loyalty have often been linked, and patriotism has been measured by how quickly one abandons a native language and replaces it with English (Crawford, 2000; Skutnabb-Kangas & Cummins, 1988). Consequently, in U.S. classrooms, linguistic diversity has commonly been viewed as a temporary, if troublesome, barrier to learning. The thinking has been that once students learned English, learning could proceed unhampered. As a result, forgetting their native language has generally been viewed as a regrettable but necessary price to pay for the benefits of citizenship. But U.S. language policies and practices have by no means been uniform. Instead, they have ranged from "sink-or-swim" policies (i.e., immersing language-minority students in English-only classrooms where they must fend for themselves), to the imposition of English as the sole medium of instruction (sometimes with minimal English as a second language [ESL] support), all the way to allowing and even encouraging bilingualism.

The notion that students needed to lose their native language in order to succeed in school has been challenged since the 1960s, when language-minority communities began to demand bilingual education (Crawford, 2004;

García, 2001; Nieto, 2001). The struggle for bilingual education, one of many struggles that emerged from the civil rights movement, was based on the premise that teaching children in their native language would help turn around the abysmal educational outcomes that were traditional for many immigrants, particularly Latinos. As a result, from the 1960s to the 1990s, many advocates took to the streets, legislatures, and courts to advocate for bilingual education. The results can be seen in such cases as the 1974 *Lau v. Nichols*, and in such legislation as the 1968 Bilingual Education Act. In *Lau*, the U.S. Supreme Court recognized the connection between native language rights and equal educational opportunity by ruling unanimously that the civil rights of students who did not understand the language of instruction were indeed being violated. The Court's decision reads, in part:

> There is no equality of treatment merely by providing students with the same facilities, textbooks, teachers, and curriculum; for students who do not understand English are effectively foreclosed from any meaningful education. Basic skills are at the very core of what these public schools teach. Imposition of a requirement that, before a child can effectively participate in the educational program he must already have acquired those basic skills, is to make a mockery of public education. (*Lau v. Nichols*, 1974)

Although the decision did not impose any particular remedy, its impact was immediate and extensive. By 1975, the U.S. Office for Civil Rights and the Department of Health, Education, and Welfare issued a document called "The *Lau* Remedies," which served as the basis for determining whether or not school systems throughout the United States were in compliance with the *Lau* decision. Bilingual programs became the common remedy of most school systems.

Bilingual programs may also have secondary salutary effects beyond teaching children English and allowing them to retain their native language. These include motivating students to remain in school rather than dropping out and, in general, making the school experience more meaningful and enjoyable (Nieto, 2004). A related phenomenon may be that bilingual education reinforces close relationships among children and their family members, promoting better communication than if they were instructed solely in English and became less able to use their native language at home (Baker & Jones, 1998; Crawford, 2004).

Although bilingual education has generally been shown to be more effective than programs such as English immersion or ESL only in teaching English and helping students keep up academically with other subject areas, it remains controversial (Crawford, 2004; Cummins, 1996; Nieto, 2001). However, a recent literature review of related research by James Crawford (2004) confirms once again the superiority of the bilingual education approach. Based on this review, Crawford concluded that successful bilingual programs have demonstrated that students can learn through their native language while learning English *and* achieving academically. In fact, fluency in English, although necessary, is no guarantee that language-minority students will succeed in school or later in life. Alejandro Portes and Rubén Rumbaut (2001) have found that students from nationalities that speak English best (including West Indians and Filipinos) are not necessarily those who earn the highest incomes or have the highest number of managers and professionals among their ranks. Chinese and other Asians, and Colombians and other Latin Americans, who have relatively low English fluency earn considerably more. Race and social status also play a key role.

The public has always been deeply divided over bilingual education, and this is truer today than ever before. Examples can be seen in California's passing of Proposition 227 in 1998, which resulted in the elimination of bilingual education, and in similar propositions in Arizona (2000) and Massachusetts (2002). These measures demonstrate a general reluctance to support bilingual education because it involves the use of languages other than English for instruction. The fact that one of the fundamental goals of bilingual education is the learning of English often goes unmentioned by opponents, who may perceive using languages of instruction other than English as a threat to national unity. But the myth that English has been a unifying force is just that. James Crawford (2000), who has exhaustively researched language policies in the United States, has suggested that such notions obscure a multilingual tradition unsurpassed in its variety while also inventing a unifying role for English that it has rarely enjoyed.

—Multicultural Education

The history of what is now known as multicultural education is a long one, beginning early in the twentieth century with calls for the improvement of education among African Americans (Du Bois, 2001; Woodson, 1933). A precursor to multicultural education was the intergroup and intercultural education movement that began in the late 1920s and lasted until the late 1950s (C. Banks, 2004). These movements were the first educational attempts to acknowledge the multiracial and multicultural character of the United States by incorporating curriculum and material that promoted intercultural understanding and respect. But multicultural education as we now know it began in the early 1970s, and it too — like desegregation and bilingual education — emerged from the civil rights movement.

Multicultural education covers a broad range of approaches and definitions (Banks & Banks, 2004). Nevertheless, most proponents agree that it is based on the need to provide all students with a high-quality and equitable education. This is particularly crucial for those students who have been failed by the public schools because of differences such as race/ethnicity, language, immigrant status, social class, and others that are often positioned negatively in society. Besides affirming the identities of all students through a more inclusive curriculum and culturally responsive pedagogy, multicultural education also takes into account the sociopolitical context in which education takes place by challenging institutional policies and practices, both in schools and society, that perpetuate inequality. As such, it is part of comprehensive school reform and a project in the larger struggle for social justice (Nieto, 2004). For example, the growing research on inequality in education begun in the 1960s and continuing through the present has highlighted the deleterious effects of such policies as tracking (Oakes, 1985), inequitable funding (Kozol, 1991), testing (Neill, 1997), and others.

As a result, from the beginning, multicultural education was viewed as a way to achieve the elusive goal of an equal educational opportunity for students of all backgrounds and circumstances. Consequently, it was based on a number of premises: that all children bring resources and strengths to their learning; that racism and other individual and institutional biases frequently get in the way of an equitable education; that other societal and school environments and structures can also hinder learning; that acknowledging and supporting the cultures, backgrounds, and communities of all children can be a positive ingredient in their education; and that schools can become places of affirmation and success for all children.

Christine Sleeter and Carl Grant (1987), in an early and influential analysis of the field published in the *Harvard Educational Review,* identified five approaches to multicultural education: *teaching the culturally different,* based on the notion that instruction needs to be adapted for students who are different from "mainstream" or dominant group students; *human relations,* an approach that emphasizes the need to treat all people fairly and equitably; *single-group studies,* in which one specific ethnic or racial group is the basis of study; *multicultural education,* an approach that acknowledges and celebrates the differences that students bring to their education; and *education that is multicultural and social reconstructionist,* an approach to transform an entire educational program while critiquing social structures and encouraging students to take an active stance in changing them. Although these versions of multicultural education often have competing aims and approaches, from the beginning of its development all advocates have agreed that multicultural education in any form was a more hopeful approach than the monocultural education that was in place in most schools. Moreover, according to Patricia Ramsey and Leslie Williams (2003), while many practitioners have initially been attracted to the "teaching the culturally different" approach, their experiences eventually lead them to embrace a more critical stance in which they begin to question institutional policies that discriminate against some students based on their social and cultural identities.

To counter the tendency to focus on superficial approaches to multicultural education in schools, James Banks (1991) developed what he called the *dimensions of multicultural education.* The dimensions include content integration, the extent to which content from a variety of cultures and groups is integrated into the curriculum; knowledge construction, the extent to which teachers and students understand how the perspectives, biases, and frames of reference in particular disciplines help shape knowledge in those disciplines; prejudice reduction, the way in which teachers help students develop positive and anti-biased attitudes about people of different backgrounds; equity pedagogy, in which pedagogical strategies are modified to help students of all backgrounds learn effectively; and empowering school culture and social structure, where the climate and organization of the school promote an equitable learning environment. These dimensions have been significant in defining the field, and they have led to the understanding that institutional changes in policies and practices are needed if multicultural education is to be a true and lasting reform. Thus, the "heroes and holidays" approach — characterized by such events as diversity dinners, celebrations of various nations or ethnicities, and other activities that do not consider the effects of structural inequality — has come under increasing criticism in the past decade (Bigelow, Christensen, Karp, Miner, & Peterson, 1994; Bigelow, Harvey, Karp, & Miller, 2001; Lee, Menkart, & Okazawa-Rey, 1998; Nieto, 2004).

Multicultural education has undergone a number of changes since its inception three decades ago. According to Ramsey and Williams (2003), two major changes are a broadening of the scope of multicultural education to include issues other than race and ethnicity, and a new focus on the identities and assumptions of White people and how these become normalized, to the detriment of others, throughout schools and society. The incorporation of critical pedagogy as a central tenet of multicultural education has also had a major impact on the field in several important ways: it affirms students' cultures without trivializing them by focusing on deeper dynamics of cultures rather than on surface characteristics; it challenges hegemonic knowledge; it complicates pedagogy so that there is no longer just one right way to teach; it challenges the simplistic focus on self-esteem as a way to break the bonds of oppression; it encourages "dangerous discourses" (Bigler, 1999, p. 119) that name and challenge inequities; and it recognizes that multicultural education is not a panacea for the problems of stratification and alienation (Nieto, 1999). In these ways, multicultural education has helped to challenge the assumption that all children have an equal chance at an excellent education, and it has been a cornerstone of the "high hopes" reflected in the title of this article.

In the final analysis, the multicultural education movement reflects the need to view school reform in a more comprehensive way. Rather than simply replacing some bureaucratic structures with others, multicultural education challenges the very structures themselves by suggesting that school policies and practices help create, maintain, and perpetuate inequality in the first place.

Broken Promises

Unfortunately, our public schools have never quite lived up to the high hopes envisioned by Mann and Dewey. In spite of John Dewey's (1916) idealistic assertion that "it is the aim of progressive education to take part in correcting unfair privilege and unfair deprivation, not to perpetuate them" (pp. 119-120), schools have too often served to uphold privilege. While the history of U.S. schools has been distinguished by the struggle for equality and by great moments of social justice and inclusion, it has also been characterized by segregation, exclusion, and racism.

School segregation has become an endemic problem in U.S. schools, reflecting residential and other patterns of social segregation. Regardless of the growing diversity in schools around the country, and despite the desegregation movement that began over fifty years ago, racial and ethnic segregation is on the rise. Students in U.S. schools are now more likely to be segregated from students of other races and backgrounds than at any time in the recent past. In fact, according to researcher Gary Orfield (2001), for Blacks, the 1990s witnessed the largest backward movement toward segregation since the 1954 *Brown v. Board of Education* decision, and the trend is continuing. Moreover, Latinos now have the dubious distinction of being the most segregated of all ethnic groups in terms of race, ethnicity, and poverty (Orfield & Yun, 1999).

Bilingual education has also been greatly dismantled. The 1968 Bilingual Education Law has been quietly, but almost completely, taken apart, and now emphasizes only English-language acquisition. And although fully forty-three states and the District of Columbia have legislative provisions for students with limited English proficiency, the number of students in bilingual classrooms has decreased over the past several years. In 2000, for instance, only 19 percent of language-minority students were receiving any instruction in their native language (Kindler, 2002). One reason is that bilingual education has been eliminated in a number of states since the late 1990s, often because of an entrenched ideological resistance to approaches based on native-language instruction.

Multicultural education too has been tremendously controversial since its beginnings. Reflecting as it does an opposition to a hegemonic education, and because it has been viewed by the Right as a threat to a common U.S. culture and by the Left as little more than "ethnic cheerleading," multicultural education has been criticized from all sides (Nieto, 1995; Sleeter, 1995). Yet the goals of multicultural education, when viewed within the context of a democratic society, have the potential to expand opportunities rather than limit them. According to Amy Gutmann (2004), "Multicultural education in democracies can help further civic equality in two important different ways: first, by expressing the democratic value of tolerating cultural differences that are consistent with civic quality, and second, by recognizing the role that cultural differences played in shaping society and the world in which children live" (p. 71).

The reemergence of extraordinarily segregated schools, the almost total dismantling of bilingual education, and the continuing vociferous backlash against multicultural education are vivid indications of the widespread resistance to social change in U.S. public education. As a result of the difficulties that these movements have had in becoming institutionalized or even accepted by the general public as essential to equalize the playing field for all children, the future of such efforts is uncertain.

Conclusion: An Uncertain Future

In our nation, access to an equal and high-quality education has long been regarded as the birthright of all children, regardless of station or rank. However, in spite of this cherished ideal, our educational history — as we have seen in this essay — is replete with examples of grossly uneven access and outcomes. These discrepancies are more often than not related to students' race/ethnicity, social class, gender, and other differences, and they are not new. Francesco Cordasco (1973, 1998), writing more than a quarter of a century ago, described the inequality in U.S. schools in this way: "In a multi-racial, ethnically variegated society, the American experience (certainly in its schools) has been an experience of cultural assault, discriminatory rejection of educational opportunity for many children, and the continuation of social and economic advantage for a white Anglo-Saxon, Protestant, middle-class patrician elite" (p. 4). Many years later, Henry Giroux (1992), echoing this theme, characterized the situation in public education as "a retreat from democracy," an apt description for a system that was supposed to be at the core of democratic values.

In this article, I have argued that public education in the United States during the past seventy-five years has been the front line of the larger battle for equality and social justice. While many smaller skirmishes have been won, the outcome of the larger struggle is uncertain and, in some ways, it is in greater jeopardy than ever. The struggle has not been easy because public education has reflected both the high ideals of equality and the limited vested interests that challenge those high ideals; this tension has been critically evident in the area of race. According to educational historian David Tyack (1995), "Attempts to preserve white supremacy and to achieve racial justice have fueled the politics of education for more than a century" (p. 4). In spite of our society's passionate ideology of equality, as a nation we have a long way to go in reaching this goal.

The current policy climate at both the state and national levels is permeated by a profound distrust for public education and for teacher education, especially when the schools in question are for poor children (Cochran-Smith, 2003; Nieto, 2003). In spite of the rhetoric of equal education for all, there is no level playing field for children in our country, a situation that was vividly demonstrated a number of years ago by Jonathan Kozol's (1991) groundbreaking exposé of the discrepancies between urban and suburban schools. In his study, Kozol demonstrated that schools, sometimes adjacent to one another geographically, are as different as night and day in terms of funding and attention. Regrettably, the situation has not changed noticeably since the publication of Kozol's book; a child's zip code is still almost a sure indication of the kind of education he or she will receive. Recently, rather than being a paragon of educational equality, U.S. schools have consistently ranked among the most unequal in the industrialized world in terms of spending, curricular offerings, and teaching quality. The imbalanced support for children from different segments of society is invariably related to their social class, race, and ethnicity (Darling-Hammond, 2001).

Although education has been understood in our society as a major gateway out of poverty — and it has served this function admirably for some — academic success has been elusive for large numbers of young people who are economically poor, or culturally and racially different from the "mainstream," or both. Our schools cannot fulfill the ambitious and noble purpose they were purported to meet unless all of us — parents, policymakers, and the general public — commit ourselves to sustaining education as a public trust for future generations. It is time once again to direct our attention to the institutional and structural barriers that impede educational equality. As we commemorate the seventy-fifth anniversary of the *Harvard Educational Review*, we would do well to remember the vision articulated by such visionaries as Horace Mann (1868), John Dewey (1916), W.E. B. Du Bois (2001), George Sanchez (1940), and other advocates of public education, because it is far from evident today. What will it take for our schools to become the beacon of hope that they once were? I believe it will take committing the nation's *full* moral and economic resources to all schools and students, but particularly to those who have been most jeopardized by broken promises. Our response to this dilemma may well determine the future of public education in our nation.

References

Alvarez, R. R., Jr. (1986). The Lemon Grove incident: The nation's first successful desegregation court case. *Journal of San Diego History, 32,* 116–135.

Anderson, J. D. (1988). *The education of Blacks in the south, 1869–1935.* Chapel Hill: University of North Carolina Press.

Anyon, J. (1981). Social class and school knowledge. *Curriculum Inquiry, 11*(1), 3–41.

Apple, M. W. (1986). *Teachers and texts: A political economy of class and gender relations in education.* Boston: Routledge-Kegan Paul.

Archuleta, M. L., Child, B. J., & Lomawaima, K. T. (2000). *Away from home: American Indian boarding school experiences, 1879–2000.* Phoenix: Heard Museum.

Au, K. H. (1980). Participant structures in a reading lesson with Hawaiian children. *Anthropology and Education Quarterly, 11*(2), 91–115.

Baker, C., & Jones, S. P. (1998). *Encyclopedia of bilingualism and bilingual education.* Clevedon, Eng.: Multilingual Matters.

Banks, C. A. M. (2004). *Improving multicultural education: Lessons from the Intergroup Education movement.* New York: Teachers College Press.

Banks, J. A. (1991). The dimensions of multicultural education. *Multicultural Leader, 4,* 5–6.

Banks, J. A. (2004). Multicultural education: Historical development, dimensions, and practice. In J. A. Banks & C. A. M. Banks (Eds.), *Handbook of research on multicultural education* (pp. 3–29). San Francisco: Jossey-Bass.

Banks, J. A., & Banks, C. A. M. (Eds.). (2004). *Handbook of research on multicultural education* (2nd ed.). San Francisco: Jossey-Bass.

Baratz, S. S., & Baratz, J. C. (1970). Early childhood intervention: The social science base of institutional racism. *Harvard Educational Review, 40,* 29–50.

Bereiter, C., & Englemann, S. (1966). *Teaching disadvantaged children in the preschool.* Englewood Cliffs, NJ: Prentice-Hall.

Bigelow, B., Christensen, L., Karp, S., Miner, B., & Peterson, B. (Eds.). (1994). *Rethinking our classrooms: Teaching for equity and justice* (vol. 1). Milwaukee: Rethinking Schools.

Bigelow, B., Harvey, B., Karp, S., & Miller, L. (Eds.). (2001). *Rethinking our classrooms: Teaching for equity and justice* (vol. 2). Milwaukee: Rethinking Schools.

Bigler, E. (1999). *American conversations: Puerto Ricans, White ethnics, and multicultural education.* Philadelphia: Temple University Press.

Bowles, S., & Gintis, H. (1976). *Schooling in capitalist America: Economic reform and the contradictions of economic life.* New York: Basic Books.

Brown v. Board of Educ., 347 U.S. 483 (1954).

Cochran-Smith, M. (2002). Editorial: Reporting on teacher quality: The politics of politics. *Journal of Teacher Education, 53*(5).

Cordasco, F. (1998). America and the quest for equal educational opportunity: The schools and the children of the poor. *Selected documents in social policy.* New York: Edna Vaughn. (Reprinted from *British Journal of Educational Studies, 21,* February, 1973, 0–63)

Crawford, J. (2000). *At war with diversity: U.S. language policy in an age of anxiety.* Clevedon, Eng.: Multilingual Matters.

Crawford, J. (2004). *Educating English learners: Language diversity in the classroom.* Los Angeles: Bilingual Education Services.

Cummins, J. (1996). *Negotiating identities: Education for empowerment in a diverse society.* Ontario: California Association for Bilingual Education.

Darling-Hammond, L. (2001). *The right to learn: A blueprint for creating schools that work.* San Francisco: Jossey-Bass.

Del Rio Independent School District v. Salvatierra, 33 S. W. 2d 790 (Texas 1930).

Dewey, J. (1916). *Democracy and education.* New York: Free Press.

Donato, R. (1997). *The other struggle for equal schools: Mexican Americans during the civil rights movement.* Albany: State University of New York Press.

Du Bois, W. E. B., & Aptheker, H. (2001). *The education of Black people: Ten critiques 1906–1960.* New York: Monthly Review Press.

Erickson, F. (1993). Transformation and school success: The politics and culture of educational achievement. In E. Jacob & C. Jordan (Eds.), *Minority education: Anthropological perspectives* (pp. 27–51). Norwood, NJ: Ablex.

Fine, M. (1991). *Framing dropouts: Notes on the politics of an urban high school.* Albany: State University of New York Press.

Flores-González, N. (2002). *School kids, street kids: Identity and high school completion among Latinos.* New York: Teachers College Press.

Fordham, S., & Ogbu, J. U. (1986). Black students' school success: Coping with the "burden of acting White." *Urban Review, 18,* 176–206.

García, E. E. (2001). *Hispanic education in the United States: Raíces y alas.* New York: Rowman & Littlefield.

Gay, G. (2000). *Culturally responsive teaching: Theory, research, and practice.* New York: Teachers College Press.

Giroux, H. A. (1983). *Theory and resistance in education: A pedagogy for the opposition.* South Hadley, MA: Bergin & Garvey.

Giroux, H. A. (1992). Educational leadership and the crisis of democratic government. *Educational Researcher, 21*(4), 4–11.

Gutmann, A. (2004). Unity and diversity in democratic multicultural education: Creative and destructive tensions. In J. A. Banks (Ed.), *Diversity and citizenship education* (pp. 71–96). San Francisco: Jossey-Bass.

Heath, S. B. (1983). *Ways with words.* New York: Cambridge University Press.

Jensen, A. R. (1969). How much can we boost IQ and scholastic achievement? *Harvard Educational Review, 39,* 1–123.

Katz, M. B. (1975). *Class, bureaucracy, and the schools: The illusion of educational change in America*. New York: Praeger.

Kindler, A. L. (2002). *Survey of the states' limited English proficient students and available educational programs and services, 1999–2000 summary report*. Washington, DC: U.S. Department of Education, Office of English Language Acquisition, Language Enhancement, and Academic Achievement for Limited English Proficient Students.

Kohl, H. (1994). *"I won't learn from you" and other thoughts on creative maladjustment*. New York: New Press.

Kozol, J. (1991). *Savage inequalities: Children in America's schools*. New York: Crown.

Ladson-Billings, G. (1994). *The dreamkeepers: Successful teachers of African American children*. San Francisco: Jossey-Bass.

Ladson-Billings, G. (2004). Landing on the wrong note: The price we paid for *Brown*. *Educational Researcher, 33*(7), 3–13.

Lau v. Nichols, 414 U.S. 563 (1974).

Lee, E., Menkart, D., & Okazawa-Rey, M. (1998). *Beyond heroes and holidays: A practical guide to K–12 anti-racist, multicultural education and staff development*. Washington, DC: Teaching for Change.

Mann, H. (1868). Twelfth annual report to the Massachusetts State Board of Education, 1848. In M. Mann (Ed.), *Life and works of Horace Mann* (vol. 3, p. 669). Boston: Walker, Fuller.

McBeth, S. (1983). *Ethnic identity and the boarding school experience of west-central Oklahoma American Indians*. Washington, DC: University Press of America.

McDermott, R. P. (1977). Social relations as contexts for learning in school. *Harvard Educational Review, 47*(2), 198–213.

National Center for Education Statistics. (2002). State nonfiscal survey of public elementary/secondary education, 2000–2001. *Common Core of Data (CCD)*.

Neill, M. (1997). *Testing our children: A report card on state assessment systems*. Cambridge, MA: FairTest.

Nieto, S. (1995). From Brown heroes and holidays to assimilationist agendas: Reconsidering the critiques of multicultural education. In C. E. Sleeter & P. L. McLaren (Eds.), *Multicultural education, critical pedagogy, and the politics of difference* (pp. 191–220). Albany: State University of New York Press.

Nieto, S. (1999). Critical multicultural education and students' perspectives. In S. May (Ed.), *Rethinking multicultural and antiracist education: Towards critical multiculturalism* (pp. 191–215). London: Falmer Press.

Nieto, S. (2001). We speak in many tongues: Linguistic diversity and multicultural education. In C. P. Díaz (Ed.), *Multicultural education for the twenty-first century* (pp. 152–170). New York: Longman.

Nieto, S. (2003). *What keeps teachers going?* New York: Teachers College Press.

Nieto, S. (2004). *Affirming diversity: The sociopolitical context of multicultural education* (4th ed.). Boston: Allyn & Bacon.

Noddings, N. (1992). *The challenge to care in schools: An alternative approach to education*. New York: Teachers College Press.

Oakes, J. (1985). *Keeping track: How schools structure inequality*. New Haven, CT: Yale University Press.

Ogbu, J. U. (1987). Variability in minority school performance: A problem in search of an explanation. *Anthropology and Education Quarterly, 18*, 312–334.

Orfield, G. (2001). *Schools more separate: Consequences of a decade of resegregation*. Cambridge, MA: Civil Rights Project at Harvard University.

Orfield, G., & Yun, J. T. (1999). *Resegregation in American schools*. Cambridge, MA: Civil Rights Project at Harvard University.

Pang, V. O., Kiang, P. N., & Pak, Y. K. (2004). Asian Pacific American students. In J. A. Banks & C. A. M. Banks (Eds.), *Handbook of research on multicultural education* (2nd ed., pp. 542–563). San Francisco: Jossey-Bass.

Portes, A., & Rumbaut, R. G. (2001). *Legacies: The story of the immigrant second generation.* Berkeley: University of California Press.

Ramsey, P. G., & Williams, L. R. (2003). *Multicultural education: A source book* (2nd ed.) New York: Routledge Falmer.

Reissman, F. (1962). *The culturally deprived child.* New York: Harper & Row.

Ruiz, V. L. (2001). South by southwest: Mexican Americans and segregated schooling: 1900–1950. *Magazine of History, 15*(2), 23–27.

Ryan, W. (1972). *Blaming the victim.* New York: Vintage Books.

Sánchez, G. I. (1940). *Forgotten people: A study of New Mexicans.* Albuquerque: University of New Mexico Press.

San Miguel, G., Jr. (2001). *Brown, not White: School integration and the Chicano movement in Houston.* College Station: Texas A & M University Press.

Siddle Walker, V. (1996). *Their highest potential: An African American community school in the segregated south.* Chapel Hill: University of North Carolina Press.

Skutnabb-Kangas, T., & Cummins, J. (Eds.). (1988). *Minority education: From shame to struggle.* Clevedon, Eng.: Multilingual Matters.

Sleeter, C. E. (1995). An analysis of the critiques of multicultural education. In J. A. Banks & C. A. M. Banks (Eds.), *Handbook of research on multicultural education* (pp. 81–94). New York: Macmillan.

Sleeter, C. E., & Grant, C. A. (1987). An analysis of multicultural education in the United States. *Harvard Educational Review, 57,* 421–444.

Spring, J. (1972). *The rise and fall of the corporate state.* Boston: Beacon Press.

Spring, J. (2004). Deculturalization and the struggle for equality: A brief history of the education of dominated cultures in the United States (4th ed.). New York: McGraw-Hill.

Stanton-Salazar, R. (1997). A social capital framework for understanding the socialization of racial minority children and youth, *Harvard Educational Review, 67,* 1–40.

Steele, C. M. (2004). A threat in the air: How stereotypes shape intellectual identity and performance. In J. A. Banks & C. A. M. Banks (Eds.), *Handbook of research on multicultural education* (pp. 682–698). San Francisco: Jossey-Bass.

Suárez-Orozco, C., & Suárez-Orozco, M. (2001). *Children of immigration.* Cambridge, MA: Harvard University Press.

Tyack, D. (1995). Schooling and social diversity: Historical reflections. In W. D. Hawley & A. W. Jackson (Eds.), *Toward a common destiny: Improving race and ethnic relations in America* (pp. 3–38). San Francisco: Jossey-Bass.

U.S. Census Bureau. (2000a). *USA Statistics in brief: Population and vital statistics.* Washington, DC: U.S. Department of Commerce. Available online at http://www.census.gov/statab/www/popppart.htm..

U.S. Census Bureau. (2000b). *Poverty in the United States: 2000.* Washington, DC: U.S. Government Printing Office.

U.S. Census Bureau. (2002). *Profile of the foreign-born population in the United States: 2000.* Washington, DC: U.S Department of Commerce.

Valenzuela, A. (1999). *Subtractive schooling: U.S.-Mexican youth and the politics of caring.* Albany: State University of New York Press.

Weinberg, M. A. (1977). *A chance to learn: A history of race and education.* Cambridge, Eng.: Cambridge University Press.

Westminster School District of Orange County v. Mendez, 161 F. 2d 774 (9th Cir. 1947).

Willis, J. S., Lintz, A., & Mehan, H. (2004). Ethnographic studies of multicultural education in U.S. classrooms and schools. In J. A. Banks & C. A. M. Banks (Eds.), *Handbook of research on multicultural education* (2nd ed., pp. 163–183). San Francisco: Jossey-Bass.

Woodson, C. G. (1933). *The mis-education of the Negro.* Washington, DC: Associated Publishers.

I am grateful to the editors of the *Harvard Educational Review* for their thoughtful suggestions on an earlier draft of this article, and to Patty Bode for invaluable editorial assistance.

What "Counts" as Educational Policy? Notes toward a New Paradigm

JEAN ANYON
City University of New York

In my first article as a young PhD, which was published in the *Harvard Educational Review*, I argued that high school U.S. history curriculum, as represented in widely used textbooks, excises and thereby defines out of existence radical responses American workers have had to the problems they face on the job and in their communities (Anyon, 1979). This educational excision is one way that schooling mitigates against the development of working-class consciousness.

In empirical and theoretical work since then, I have investigated knowledge and pedagogical experiences made available to students in different social-class contexts (1980, 1981), and have attempted to understand the consequences of ways we conceptualize urban education, urban school reform, and neighborhood poverty. Recent arguments have aimed at unseating simplistic notions of the causes of urban poverty and low achievement in city districts, and explicating unexplored relations between urban education and movements for social change (e.g., 1995, 1997, 2005).

In this chapter I think about education policy over the seventy-five years of *Harvard Educational Review* publication. During these decades, many K–12 policies have been written and implemented by federal, state, and local governments. Some of these have aimed at improving education in America's cities and are my primary focus. Over the years, dominant strategies called upon to improve urban schools have included curricular, administrative, and funding reforms, as well as increases in educational opportunity and district/school accountability.

A historical examination of policies can inform decisions we make today. Policy failures, for example, may demonstrate that we need to rethink strategies we choose in our long-term attempts to solve the problems of school and student achievement in urban districts. Indeed, I will argue that the quality of education in city schools is a complex problem, and education policy as historically conceived has not been adequate to the task of increasing urban school achievement to acceptable levels. Academic learning in city schools is undoubtedly higher than in, say, 1900, yet there is still no large urban district that can demonstrate high achievement in even half its students or schools. Noting this failure of educational policy to render most urban schools high-quality institutions, I ask, what *should* count as educational policy? As in any attempt to resolve complex issues, workable solutions can only be generated by an understanding of underlying causes.

The diagnosis I provide is based on analyses completed for my book, *Radical Possibilities: Public Policy, Urban Education, and a New Social Movement* (Anyon, 2005). In this book I examine federal and regional mandates that affect economic and social opportunities available to the urban poor. I find that despite stated intentions, federal and metropolitan policies and arrangements generally restrict opportunities available to city residents and neighborhoods. I show how job, wage, housing, tax, and transportation policies maintain minority poverty in urban neighborhoods, and thereby create environments that overwhelm the potential of educational policy to create systemic, sustained improvements in the schools. For example, policies such as minimum wage statutes that yield full-time pay below the poverty level, and affordable housing and transportation policies that segregate low-income workers of color in urban areas but industrial and other job development in far-flung suburbs where public transit routes do not reach, are all culpable.

In order to solve the systemic problems of urban education, then, I argue in the book — and will argue here — that we need not only better schools but also the reform of these public policies. Rules and regulations regarding teaching, curriculum, and assessment certainly are important, but policies to eliminate poverty-wage work and housing segregation (for example) should be part of the educational policy panoply as well, for these have consequences for urban education at least as profound as curriculum, pedagogy, and testing.

In the sections that follow I describe major K–12 education policies that have been implemented over the years to attempt to improve urban education, and then discuss several federal and metro-area policies and practices that limit the potential and success of these strategies. I also report hopeful new research suggesting that even modest income and other family supports typically improve low-income students' academic achievement. I end by arguing that, given this power of economic access to influence educational outcomes, strategies to support economic opportunity and development for urban residents and neighborhoods should be among the policies we consider in our attempts to improve urban schools and districts. Just as in affluent suburban districts where economic strength is the engine of educational reform, so it would be in urban districts where resident and neighborhood affluence would support and retool the schools. I begin with an overview of education policy as typically conceived.

Education Policies

Over the last seventy-five years or so, federal policies have attempted various strategies to improve city education. The first federal policy aimed at working-class populations was the Smith-Hughes Act of 1917, which provided funds to prepare students in industrialized areas for working-class jobs through vocational programs. Variants of this policy continued throughout the twentieth century, in the Vocational Education Acts of 1963, 1984, and 1998, and in the School-to-Work Opportunity Act of 1994 and the later federal legislation in which it was subsumed.

Some federal education policies have attempted to improve urban education by making funding available for increased curriculum materials and libraries, early childhood classes, and various types of programmatic innovations in city schools. Head Start in 1965, Follow Through in 1967, and, to a lesser extent, Title IX, which banned sex discrimination in 1972, brought and instigated new curricula and programs into city districts.[1] These policies were intended to increase student access and/or achievement by upgrading curricular resources and experiences.

Other federal K–12 policies have aimed specifically at increasing educational equity. The 1954 *Brown* decision (which committed the federal government to desegregation as a policy stance), the Elementary and Secondary Education Act of 1965 (ESEA), the Bilingual Act in 1968, Title IX in 1972, and the Education for All Handicapped Children Act in 1975 opened doors to academic experiences for previously underserved K–12 students. These policies are generally thought to have expanded urban students' educational opportunities.

More recent federal education policies to improve schooling — with urban students and teachers often a target — have called for increased academic standards and requirements, standardized testing, and professional development of teachers. These policies were recommended by the influential report *A Nation at Risk*, commissioned by President Ronald Reagan and published in 1983. The emphasis on increased academic standards was part of an effort to support business needs for well-prepared workers and employees. The report's recommendations for higher standards and increased testing were introduced as policy in 1994 and 1996 as part of the Goals 2000 legislation. In 2001 these goals were instantiated as federal mandates in the No Child Left Behind Act (NCLB). Privatization of education via nonpublic providers when K–12 schools fail is a subtextual education policy in NCLB (Conley, 2003; Cross, 2004; Stein, 2004).

It is important to note that federal education policies intended to improve urban schools did not take aim at the economic arrangements and practices that themselves produced the poverty in which city schools were embedded. Despite increases in educational opportunity, the effects of almost a century of educational policies on urban school and student achievement have, by most accounts, been disappointing.

The first state policies regarding the education of America's urban (and rural) poor emerged earlier than federal ones. What has counted as state education policy regarding poor students can be said to have begun with mid- to late-nineteenth century insertions into state constitutions of the right of all students to a free, "thorough," "efficient," or "useful" education (Odden & Picus, 1992). Following these insertions and until the 1970s, however, most state education policies did not focus specifically on urban education. State mandates typically set regulations and requirements for school systems, teacher and administrator preparation, and school funding (through property taxes). During the 1970s and 1980s, lawsuits challenging state education funding systems brought increased attention to city schools and districts. State urban education policy in these decades involved various kinds of efforts, including school-based management and basic skills mandates. In the 1990s, state policies attempted to align education standards and regulations with federal ones, mandated curriculum and teacher licensure reform, and closely monitored urban districts. As legal challenges to state systems have led to increased funding of city schools, states have imposed stricter academic and graduation requirements, as well as multigrade and multisubject standardized testing. Quasi-privatization policies supporting charter schools, vouchers, and other school choice programs have also been a state strategy to attempt to improve the education of urban children by offering them a choice of schools to attend (Conley, 2003).

Over the decades, federal and state policies codified an increasing number of requirements that urban schools and districts must meet. Local governments and educational bureaucracies have undertaken a plethora of programs to attempt to meet those guidelines. Local districts have also mounted school reform projects in response to local social conditions and political pressure from parents and communities. Most local initiatives have been curricular, pedagogical, and administrative.

During the Progressive Era, cities consolidated and professionalized their school systems and personnel, introduced programs like the Gary Plan to prepare students for the industrial experience, increased access to high school, organized educational opportunities for immigrant parents, and sometimes fed, bathed, and clothed poor children. During the decade of the Great Depression, most large cities retrenched and severely cut educational social service and academic programs, as local tax receipts plummeted and banks that offered loans demanded broad cuts in education. During the 1960s, many urban districts were weakened further as most remaining businesses and jobs moved to the suburbs, decimating the urban property tax base (Anyon, 1997; Ravitch, 2000; Tyack, 1974; Wrigley, 1982).

Since the 1970s, in response to federal, judicial, and state mandates, urban districts have bused students to meet racial integration guidelines, decentralized authority to increase community participation, and created magnet schools to attempt to attract middle-class parents. Other local policies that have been attempted to improve achievement are a multitude of reform programs or "school improvement projects," student retention services, privatization of educational offerings, vouchers and magnets, mayoral control, small schools, and curriculum standardization and evaluation through testing. The social context of these policies has included pressure to be accountable in the wake of increased funding, as well as community and corporate demands for better schools. None of the local policies has focused on the poverty of families or neighborhoods.

One way to evaluate this long run of education policy is to compare the achievement of urban students at the beginning of the twentieth and twenty-first centuries. Although achievement is higher now in that larger percentages of students remain in school past the elementary years than in 1900, I would argue that the improvement is relative and illusory. That is, while in the early twentieth century relatively few urban poor students went beyond fifth grade, the vast majority did not require further education to find employment in industries that could lead to middle-class income (Anyon, 1997; Ayres, 1909). Currently, relatively few urban poor students go past ninth grade: The graduation rates in large comprehensive inner-city high schools are abysmally low. In fourteen such New York City schools, for example, only 10 percent to 20 percent of ninth graders in 1996 graduated four years later (Fine, 2001; Greene 2001; Miao & Haney, 2004).[2] Despite the fact that low-income individuals desperately need a college degree to find decent employment, only 7 percent obtain a bachelors degree by age twenty-six (Education Trust, 2001; Mishel, Bernstein, & Schmitt, 2001). So, in relation to the needs of low-income students, urban districts fail their students with more egregious consequences now than in the early twentieth century.

Given the plethora of federal, state, and local education policies aimed at urban schools and the current widely acknowledged necessity of high-quality education for all, why have most urban schools and districts not been able to provide such an education for their students?

Barriers to High-Quality Public Education in Cities

There are multiple causes of low-quality schooling in urban areas, and education policies as heretofore conceived address only a few. Education policy has not addressed the neighborhood poverty that surrounds and invades urban schools with low expectations and cynicism. Education policy has not addressed the unemployment and joblessness of families who will have few if any resources for the further education of their children, even if they excel in K–12 classes.

And education policy — even in response to state financial challenges — has not addressed the political economy that largely determines low levels of city district funding. Taxes on wealthy families and corporations are among the lowest on record (Phillips, 2002). Business and government investment in affluent suburban job centers rather than urban areas continues to deprive poor neighborhoods of entry-level jobs and a tax base, and residents' poverty wages further diminish available funding sources (Anyon, 2005; Orfield, 2002; Rusk, 1999). These political-economic constraints on quality schooling are not challenged by current or past education policy. In most U.S. cities, the political leverage of urban parents has not been sufficient to force the funding necessary to overcome outdated buildings, broken computer labs, and overcrowded classrooms.

These economic and political conditions are the building blocks of formidable barriers to systemic, sustainable school quality. Indeed, even when urban school reform succeeds, it fails — when there are no decent jobs a diploma from a successfully reformed school or district will attract, and there is no government or familial funding sufficient for the vast majority of low-income graduates of even good urban high schools to obtain a bachelors degree.

Individual and neighborhood poverty builds walls around schools and classrooms that education policy does not penetrate or scale. In the following section I describe some of the federal and metro-area policies and arrangements that sustain these barriers.

Federal Policy

Analysts typically do not link federal policies to the maintenance of poverty, to the lack of jobs that bedevils American workers, or to the increasingly large portion of employment that pays poverty and near-poverty wages. Yet federal policy is determinative. To take a blatant example, Congress set the first minimum wage in 1938 at $3.05 (in 2000 dollars); it stands in 2005 at $5.15 — a mere two dollars more. (Yearly income at this wage is $10,712.) This sum ensures that full-time, year-round, minimum-wage work will not raise people out of poverty (Mishel, Bernstein, & Boushey, 2003). Analysis in 2004 found that minimum-wage standards directly affect the wages of 8.9 percent of the workforce (9.9 million workers); when we include those making one dollar more an hour than the minimum wage, this legislation affects the wages of as much as 18 percent of the workforce (Economic Policy Institute, 2004). Contrary to the claims of those who oppose raising the minimum wage (that an increase will force employers to fire, or hire fewer of those affected by the increase), studies of the 1990–1991 and 1996–1997 minimum-wage increases failed to find any systematic, significant job losses associated with the increases and found no evidence of negative employment effects on small businesses (Economic Policy Institute, 2004).

Almost half the workforce earns what some economists call poverty-*zone* wages (and what I define as up to and including 125% of the official poverty level; Anyon, 2005). I analyzed figures provided by the Economic Policy Institute to calculate the overall percentage of people who work full-time year round yet make wages up to and including 125 percent of the official poverty threshold needed to support a family of four at the poverty level. The analysis demonstrates that in 1999, during a very strong economy, almost half of the people at work in the United States (41.3%) earned poverty-zone wages — in 1999, $10.24/hour ($21,299/year) or less, working full-time year round (Mishel et al., 2001). Two years later, in 2001, 38.4 percent earned poverty-zone wages working full-time year round (in 2001, 125% of the poverty line was a $10.88 hourly wage; Mishel et al., 2003). This suggests that the federal minimum-wage policy is an important determinant of poverty for many millions of U.S. families.

There are other macroeconomic policies that produce hardship. These especially penalize Blacks and Latinos, the majority of whom live in segregated, low-income urban neighborhoods. These policies include the following: job training as a predominant federal antipoverty policy when there have been too few jobs for graduates; ineffective federal implementation of policies that outlaw racial discrimination in hiring and housing; regressive income taxes that charge wealthy individuals less than half the rate charged the rich during most of the first sixty years of the twentieth century, yet substantially raise the payroll taxes paid by the working poor and middle class; and corporate tax policies in recent years that allow 60 percent of large U.S. corporations to pay no federal taxes at all (and in some cases to obtain millions in rebates; Citizens for Tax Justice, 2002; Lafer, 2002; Orfield, 2002; Rusk, 1999).

These federal policies and practices contribute to personal, neighborhood, and educational poverty because they lead to the following problems: There are not enough jobs for poor families who need them; low-income families of color are concentrated in low-resourced urban neighborhoods; and when the wealthy do not contribute equitably to public expenses, funding for services like education declines and the quality of the services tends to be low.

The effects of these policies are compounded by harsh union laws and lack of federal protection for labor organizing; Federal Reserve Bank pronouncements that ignore the portion of its mandate to maintain a high level of employment; and free-trade agreements that send thousands of corporations, and their job opportunities, to other countries. These policies hurt workers of all colors — and in most sectors of the economy — as existing jobs disappear and those remaining pay lower wages, in part because they are not unionized (Anyon, 2005; Citizens for Tax Justice, 2002; Economic Policy Institute, 2002, 2004; Galbraith, 1998; Lafer, 2002; Mishel et al., 2001).

However, there are federal policies we could create that would lower poverty by important margins — including a significantly raised minimum wage, comparable worth laws, and policies to enforce existing regulations that outlaw discrimination in hiring. A raise in the minimum wage that brought workers above poverty would improve the lives of at least a fifth of U.S. workers (Economic Policy Institute, 2004). Paying women the same amount men are paid for comparable work would, according to one analysis, reduce poverty by 40 percent, as such a large percentage of poor people are women in low-wage jobs (Lafer, 2002). And requiring employers to hire without discriminating against Blacks and Latinos would further open opportunities currently denied.

In addition, policies that worked against U.S. poverty in the past could be reinstated: U.S. government regulation of the minimum wage, which kept low-paid workers' income at the median of highly paid unionized workers in the decades after World War II; federal support for union organizing; a federal program of job creation in cities, as during the Great Depression of the 1930s; and federal programs for urban youth that would support further education, as such policies did for eight million men and women after World War II (Anyon, 2005; Galbraith, 1998). These national policies were important supports of the widespread prosperity of the United States' working and middle classes in the quarter century following 1945 (Galbraith, 1998).

Metropolitan Policy and Practice

Like current federal mandates, there are metro-area policies and practices that increase the problems of urban residents and neighborhoods. Metro areas are shaped by regional markets — for jobs, housing, investment, and production. Metro areas account for over 80 percent of national output and drive the economic performance of the nation as a whole. Each metro area is anchored by one or more cities (Dreier, Mollenkopf, & Swanstrom, 2001).

Today, metropolitan regions are characterized by population growth, extensive inequality, and segregation (Orfield, 2002; Rusk, 1999). The percentage of racial minorities in large metro areas who live in the suburbs jumped from 19 percent to 27 percent during the 1990s. However, a growing share of these families lives in fiscally stressed suburbs, with an increasing number of neighborhoods having poverty levels over 30 percent (Kingsley & Petit, 2003; Orfield, 2002). As in areas of concentrated poverty in the central city, low levels of taxable resources in these "urbanized" segregated suburbs leave services like education lacking in funds.

U.S. metropolitan areas are characterized by the following problems, all of which disadvantage urban minority families and communities: Most entry-level jobs for which adults with low to moderate education levels are qualified are increasingly located in suburbs, rather than in central cities, but public transit systems do not connect these suburban job centers to urban areas, where most low-income minorities live — thus preventing them from access to

jobs there. State-allowed local zoning on the basis of income prevents affordable housing in most suburbs where entry-level jobs are located, which means
there is little if any housing for low-income families near the suburban job
centers. Indeed, as I have mentioned, the failure to enforce antiracial discrimination statutes in housing confines most Blacks and Latinos to housing sites
in central cities and segregated suburbs. Finally, even though federal and state
taxes are paid by residents throughout metro regions (including inner cities),
most tax-supported development takes place in the affluent suburbs rather
than in low-income areas. Thus, few jobs exist in most low-income urban
neighborhoods (Anyon, 2005; Dreir et al., 2001; Orfield, 2002; Rusk, 1999).
These inequitable regional arrangements and policies exacerbate federal
wage and job mandates and contribute in important ways to joblessness and
poverty in cities and urbanized suburbs, and to the low quality of investment
in services such as education there.

Poverty

One consequence of federal and regional policies regarding work, wages,
housing segregation, and transportation is that the numbers of poor people
approach the figures of 1959 — before massive urban poverty became a national issue. Although the percentages are lower now, the numbers are still
staggering: There were about as many people officially poor in 1993 (39.2
million) as in 1959 (39.4 million; Harrington, 1963). And in 2003, 35.8 million were officially poor, only 3.5 million fewer than in 1959 (Mishel et al.,
2003).

A more realistic measure of poverty than federal guidelines is that those
earning incomes up to 200 percent of the official levels are considered poor
(Bernstein, Brocht, & Spade-Aguilar, 2000; Citro & Michael, 1995; Short, Iceland, & Garner, 1999). This revised threshold is used by increasing numbers of
social scientists. A calculation of the individuals who earned less than 200 percent of the poverty level in 2001 ($17.40/hour, or $36,192/year), demonstrates a much larger percentage of poor employees than is commonly acknowledged: *84 percent of Hispanic workers, 80 percent of Black workers, and 64.3
percent of White workers made wages at or under 200 percent of the official poverty line*
(Mishel et al., 2001).

A calculation of *families* living with earnings up to 200 percent of the poverty line reveals that Black and Latino families face the greatest financial hurdles. More than 50 percent of Black and Latino families earn less than 200 percent of the poverty level, compared to only 20.3 percent of White families,
even though White families constitute a slight majority (50.5%) of families
that fall below 200 percent of the poverty level (Mishel et al., 2001). In sum,
poverty in the United States is higher than commonly perceived and is maintained in urban areas by federal and metro-area policies and distributions.

Effects of Poverty on Urban Students

Macroeconomic policies that set wages below poverty levels, that train inner-city hopefuls for jobs that do not exist, that do not extract from the wealthy a fair share of social expenses, and that rarely enforce laws that would substantially decrease the economic discrimination of people of color all support persistent poverty and near-poverty among minority urban populations. This economic and social distress can prevent children from developing their full potential and can certainly dampen the enthusiasm, effort, and expectations with which urban children and their families approach K–12 education.

As I will report, a recent national study of young children confirms the potential of impoverished circumstances to prevent students' full cognitive growth before they enroll in kindergarten. Of countervailing power, however, is research demonstrating that when parents obtain better financial resources or better living conditions, the educational achievement of the children typically improves significantly. These findings empirically support the argument that for the urban poor, even with the right educational policies in place, school achievement may await a family's economic access.

I already presented adult poverty figures at the official threshold and noted the alarming increase in numbers when a more realistic assessment is made. The same disparities exist between federal and alternative counts of poor children. Sixteen percent of American children — almost 12 million — lived below the *official* federal poverty line in 2001. Almost half of those children (44%, or a little over 5 million) lived in *extreme* poverty (less than half the poverty line, or $7,400 for a family of three in 2001) — including nearly a million African American children. This was a 17 percent increase in the number of children in extreme poverty from 2000, at the end of the economic boom (Cauthen & Lu, 2001; Dillon, 2003; Lu, 2003).

When the more appropriate alternative poverty threshold criterion is applied, however, a full *38 percent* of American children are identified as poor — 27 million who lived in families with income up to 200 percent of the official poverty line. These children live in poverty as well — although official statistics do not designate them as such. However, these families experience hardships that are almost as severe as those who are officially poor (Cauthen & Lu 2001; Lu, 2003). *By the revised measure — 200 percent of the official poverty cutoff — a full 57 percent of African American children, 64 percent of Latino, and 34 percent of White children were poor in the United States in 2001* (Lu, 2003; Mishel et al., 2003).

It is only in the 1990s that empirical studies focused on why and how poverty affects cognitive development and school achievement. Researchers began to document the specific effects of poverty environments on children's development (Brooks-Gunn, Duncan, Leventhal, & Aber, 1997; Goering & Feins, 2003; Sampson, Morenoff, & Gannon-Rowley, 2002). This body of work documents the correlations between low income, child development, and educational achievement (see Duncan & Brooks-Gunn, 1997, for an overview of studies). For example, poverty has been found to have consistently negative effects on children's cognitive development (Duncan & Brooks-Gunn, 1997; Duncan, Brooks-Gunn, & Klebanov, 1994; McLoyd, 1998). Longitudinal studies that have been carried out also demonstrate that "family income consistently predicts children's academic and cognitive performance, even when other family characteristics are taken into account" (Duncan & Brooks-Gunn, 1997). Persistent and extreme poverty has been shown to be more detrimental to children than temporary poverty (Bolger & Patterson, 1995; Duncan et al., 1994). Family income may influence children through both lack of resources and parental emotional stress (Bradley, 1984; McLoyd & Jartayne, 1994; Smith, Brooks-Gunn, & Klebanov, 1997; Sugland, Zaslow, Brooks-Gunn, & Moore, 1995). Poor children have more health and behavior difficulties than those from more affluent families, which mitigates against educational success (Duncan & Brooks-Gunn, 1997; Houser, Brown, & Prosser, 1997; Klerman, 1991/2003; Korenman & Miller, 1997). Studies collected by Duncan and Brooks-Gunn teased out some of the variables within the effects of income. In summarizing research reported in their 1997 volume *Consequences of Growing up Poor*, they point out the following:

1. Income matters for the cognitive development of preschoolers "because it is associated with the provision of a richer learning environment" (p. 601). This is true in part because family income is a "significant determinant of child care environments, including center-based childcare (p. 601). . . . Income allows parents to provide their children with safer, more stimulating home environments; to live in communities with better schools, parks, and libraries and more challenging peers; to afford tuition and other expenses associated with higher education; to purchase or otherwise gain access to higher-quality health care; and in many other ways to buy the things that promote the health and development of their children" (p. 14).

2. "A variety of income measures — income [relative to needs] . . . income loss, the ratio of debts to assets, and unstable work — are associated with family economic pressure" (p. 602). Economic pressure has been found to be associated with depression (and stress) in parents, which can affect parenting, and thus school achievement.

3. "Family income is usually a stronger predictor of ability and achievement outcomes than are measures of parental schooling or family structure [e.g., single parenthood]" (p. 603). Many studies have shown that children raised in low-income families score lower than children from more affluent families do on assessments of health, cognitive development, and positive behavior. "In general, the better the measure of family income and the longer the period over which it is measured, the stronger the association between the family's economic well-being and children's outcomes" (p. 14).

It is important to understand that these findings do not suggest that poor students are of low intelligence; rather, the studies point to the power of the economy — and of economic hardship — to place extremely high hurdles to full development in front of children who are poor. It is of course possible — although it is not the norm — that education over time mitigates the effects of SES (Hout, 1988; Jencks & Phillips, 1998).

In 2002, Valerie Lee and David Burkham published the results of a large-sample assessment of the effects of poverty on cognitive development. They utilized data from the United States Department of Education's early childhood longitudinal kindergarten cohort, which is a comprehensive dataset that provides a nationally representative portrait of kindergarten students. Lee and Burkham (2002) explored differences in young children's achievement scores in literacy and mathematics by race, ethnicity, and socioeconomic status (SES) as they began kindergarten. They also analyzed differences by social background in an array of children's homes and family activities.

The study demonstrates that inequalities in children's cognitive ability by SES are substantial even before children begin kindergarten and that poverty has a detrimental impact on early intellectual achievement. Importantly, it demonstrates that the disadvantages of being poor outweigh by far the race or family structure of children as causes of the cognitive disadvantages.

Details of the national assessment include the following:

1. Before children enter kindergarten, the average cognitive scores of children in the highest SES group are 60 percent above the scores of the lowest SES group.
2. Cognitive skills are much *less* closely related to race/ethnicity after accounting for SES. After taking racial differences into account, children from different SES groups achieve at different levels — before they begin kindergarten.
3. The impact of family structure on cognitive skills (e.g., being in a single-parent family) is much less than either race or SES.
4. Socioeconomic status is very strongly related to cognitive skills; SES accounts for more of the variation in cognitive scores than any other factor by far.

Lee and Burkham (2002) also found that disadvantaged children not only enter kindergarten with significantly lower cognitive skills than their advantaged peers, but also that low-SES children begin school (kindergarten) in systematically lower-quality elementary schools than their more advantaged counterparts. "However school quality is defined — in terms of higher student achievement, more school resources, more qualified teachers, more positive teacher attitudes, better neighborhood or school conditions, private vs. public schools — the least advantaged United States children begin their formal schooling in consistently lower-quality schools. This reinforces the inequalities that develop even before children reach school age" (p. 3; see also Entwistle &

Alexander, 1997; Phillips, Brooks-Gunn, Duncan, Klevanov, & Crane, 1998; Phillips, Crouse, & Ralph, 1998; Stipic & Ryan, 1997; White, 1982).

In their review of studies of poverty's effects on individual development, Duncan and Brooks-Gunn (1997) conclude, "Taken together, [these studies] suggest that programs that raise the incomes of poor families will enhance the cognitive development of children and may improve their chance of success in [education and] the labor market during adulthood. Most important appears to be the elimination of deep and persistent poverty during a child's early years" (p. 608). I now turn to research suggesting that familial financial and other supports do indeed lead to increased educational achievement in children.

Evidence that Familial Supports Raise Educational Achievement

I have been examining relationships among education policy, the economy, and achievement in urban schools. First, I critiqued education policy for its lack of attention to urban poverty, which, I argued, is maintained by policies and decisions made at the federal and metropolitan levels. I provided evidence of some of the egregious consequences of federal and regional policies and practices for urban families, neighborhoods, students, and schools. In particular, I demonstrated that child poverty creates obstacles to full development and educational achievement, especially when low-income minority children attend low-resourced schools — which most do. In this section I provide indirect and direct research evidence that increased family supports such as financial resources and less segregated neighborhoods raise educational achievement.

Indirect evidence is present in a longitudinal study completed in 2003 that found that improving family income reduces the negative (aggressive) social behavior of children, which in turn is likely to lead to better school behavior and performance. For eight years, researchers studied a representative population sample of 1,420 children ages nine to thirteen in rural North Carolina. A quarter of the children were from a Cherokee reservation. Psychological tests were given at the start of the study and repeated each year (Costello, Compton, Keeler, & Angold, 2003; O'Connor, 2003).

When the study began, 68 percent of the children were living below the official poverty line. On average, the poorer children engaged in more vandalism, stealing, bullying, stubbornness, and outbursts of anger than those who were not poor. But halfway through the study, a local casino began distributing a percentage of its profits to tribal families. Given to each tribal member over eighteen and put in a trust fund for younger members, the payment increased slightly each year, reaching about $6,000 per person for the year 2001. Psychiatric tests administered by researchers for the four years that the funds were being distributed demonstrated that the negative behaviors of children in families who were no longer poor dropped to the same levels found among children whose families had never been poor (decreasing by 40%). Parents who moved out of poverty reported having more time to spend with their children, and researchers identified better parenting behavior. Researchers also identified the psychological benefits of not being poor as important to both parents and children. Poverty puts stress on families, which can increase the likelihood of children developing behavioral problems. One parent in the study told researchers that "the jobs [produced by the casino] give people the chance to pull themselves up by their bootstraps and get out of poverty. That carries over into less juvenile crime, less domestic violence, and an overall better living experience for families" (O'Connor, 2003, p. 2).

Other research demonstrates that urban low-income parents are also able to practice more effective parenting strategies when some of the stress of poverty is eased by a higher income. And the reduction in stress in turn may positively affect the behavior and achievement of low-income children (see information below; also Jackson, Brooks-Gunn, Huang, & Glassman, 2000; Jeremiah, 2003; Seitz, Rosenbaum, & Apfel, 1985).

Direct evidence that income supports improved educational achievement is also available. In March 2001, the Manpower Demonstration Research Corporation (MDRC) published a synthesis of research on how welfare and work policies affect the children of single mothers (Morris, Huston, Duncan, Crosby, & Bos, 2001). This synthesis reviewed data from evaluations of five programs that provided income supplements to poverty-wage workers (Florida's Family Transition Program, the Minnesota Family Investment Program, the National Evaluation of Welfare-to-Work Strategies, Milwaukee's New Hope for Families and Children Program, and the Self-Sufficiency Project). These programs offered supports of differing kinds to poverty-wage workers — income supplements, earnings disregards (rules that allow working welfare recipients to keep more of their income when they go to work), subsidized health care, employment services, counseling, supervised afterschool activities for children and youth, and informal get-togethers with project staff.

MDRC's review of the studies found that even relatively small income supplements to working parents (amounting to about $4,000 per year) improved children's elementary school achievement by about 10 to 15 percent of the average variation in the control groups. These improvements were seen on test scores as well as on ratings by parents and/or teachers. The earning supplements had "consistently positive impacts on children's [school] achievement" (Morris et al., 2001, p. 63). The positive effects were small, but were statistically significant.

Longitudinal studies have found that the achievement and behavior problems of young children can have important implications for their well-being in adolescence and adulthood (Caspi, Wright, Moffit, & Silva, 1998; Masten & Coatsworth, 1995). Moreover, even small differences between children in school achievement early on can translate into larger differences later (Entwistle & Alexander, 1997). Therefore, as the authors of the research synthesis state, "a program's effects on children, even if the effects are small, may continue to have implications over the course of their lives" (Caspi et al., 1998, p. 25).

The earning supplements provided by four of these programs did not, however, bring the families above the poverty level. The improvements in children's school achievement and behavior from even these relatively meager cash supplements for working families suggest that if we were to increase family resources substantially, we could probably improve educational and social outcomes for children substantially.

Indeed, one program that did provide an earning supplement that brought the families above poverty level showed particularly impressive results for children's behavior and achievement. New Hope for Families and Children was run between 1994 and 1998 in two inner-city areas in Milwaukee. Candidates had to live in one of two targeted areas, be eighteen or older, be willing and able to work at least thirty hours per week, and have a household income at or below 150 percent of the federal poverty level (Huston et al., 2001). Almost 90 percent of the adults in the sample were single or separated mothers with children when they entered the study, and 80 percent were receiving public assistance. The program was conceived by a nonprofit community-based organization and provided several benefits: the earnings supplement, subsidized health insurance, and subsidized child care. The program offered help in obtaining a job and provided a community-service job for up to one year for those not able to find work elsewhere, the advice and support of project staff were made available. The annual cost of providing these benefits was $5,300 per family.

New Hope was evaluated at two-year and five-year intervals using a random assignment research design. After conducting outreach in the communities to identify eligible people, the study enrolled over 1,300 low-income adults. Half the applicants were randomly assigned to a program group that received New Hope's benefits, and the other half were randomly assigned to a control group that was not eligible for the benefits.

Both evaluations showed positive results (Bos, Huston, Duncan, Brock, & McLoyd, 1996; Huston et al., 2001). Financial supplements in the New Hope program did reduce the number of families in poverty, but both program and control groups reported similar levels of hardship, such as food insecurity and financial insufficiency. Yet the program had positive effects on parents' well-being and coping skills. As Huston et al. (2003) explain:

> Parents in the New Hope group were more aware of available "helping" resources in the community, such as where to find assistance with energy costs or housing problems. More of them also knew about the [Earned Income Tax Credit] and its support, an important source of support for low-income workers. Ethnographic data suggest that a significant number of families intentionally used the Earned Income Tax Credits as a savings plan for making major purchases, reducing debt, and stabilizing rent and other payments. Parents in New

Hope also reported better physical health and fewer symptoms associated with depression than did parents in the control group. At the two-year point, New Hope parents reported reduced stress, increased feelings of social support, and increased time pressure. The ethnographic study found that many parents had children with disabilities or behavioral difficulties; New Hope helped the parents achieve a difficult balance among work, services, and parenting. . . . The New Hope parents did report fewer problems controlling their children, and parents of adolescents reported more effective management (better control and less need for punishment). (p. 9)

New Hope improved children's school performance. "At both the two-year and the five-year points, children in the program performed better than control group children on several measures of academic achievement, particularly on reading and literacy tests. After five years, they scored higher on a standardized test of reading skills and their parents reported that they got higher grades in reading skills" (Huston et al., 2001, p. 13). These effects were slightly more pronounced for boys than for girls. Compared with their control group counterparts, boys in New Hope also received higher ratings of academic performance from their teachers and were more likely to expect to attend college at both the two-year and the five-year assessments. "New Hope adolescents reported more engagement with schools, feelings of efficacy, and expectations to finish college than did their control group counterparts" (pp. 13–14). New Hope's effects are consistent with the results of other programs that have improved children's outcomes by providing wage supplements and subsidized child care (Michalopoulos et al., 2002; Morris et al., 2001).

Indeed, the New Hope findings are in line with the increased educational achievement of students that has been identified in large-scale programs that assist low-income minority families by helping them move from inner-city neighborhoods to more affluent and/or less segregated metropolitan areas. The first of these "mobility programs" was the Gautreaux program in the Chicago metropolitan area.

As a result of a victorious lawsuit charging the Chicago Housing Authority with segregation in public housing, the court ordered the housing authority to move families who wanted to live in less segregated areas of the city and suburbs. The Gautreaux program moved over 7,000 families to higher-income areas of the Chicago metropolitan region between 1976 and 1998 (Rubinowitz & Rosenbaum, 2002). Although at first a disproportionate number of the children who moved were placed in classes for the learning disabled by their suburban schools, they ultimately were significantly more likely than their urban counterparts to be in college-bound tracks, in four-year colleges, and were subsequently more likely to be employed in jobs with higher pay and with benefits than children who stayed in the city (Rubinowitz & Rosenbaum, 2002).

The success of the Gautreaux program led to more than fifty other mobility programs, including the Moving To Opportunity program (MTO) begun by the U.S. Department of Housing and Urban Development (HUD) in 1994. The Housing and Community Development Act of 1992 authorized HUD to "assist very low-income families with children who reside in public housing or housing receiving project-based assistance under Section 8 of the Housing and Community Development Act of 1937 to move out of areas with high concentrations of persons living in poverty (40% or more) to areas with low concentrations of such persons (less than 10% in poverty)" (Goering & Feins, 2003, p. 6). Moving To Opportunity projects were carried out in five cities: Baltimore, Boston, Chicago, Los Angeles, and New York. Congress stipulated that HUD conduct evaluations of the program to determine its effects (Goering & Feins, 2003).

Overall, roughly 5,300 families volunteered to move within the metropolitan area of the city in which they lived. In total, 4,608 families were eligible. They were divided into three groups: the MTO "treatment" or experimental group, which received Section 8 certificates or vouchers that could only be used in areas where 10 percent or less of the residents lived below official poverty levels; they also received counseling assistance in finding private rental units. A second group was given Section 8 certificates with no special restrictions on where they were to move, and no counseling (Section 8–only group). An in-place control group continued to receive housing project assistance in the inner-city neighborhoods where they lived. The families in all three groups of the MTO program tended to be young single mothers (under age 35), African American, with a median income of $8,200. Most stated that their main reason for wanting to move was fear of gangs and violence in the neighborhoods in which they lived.

Social scientists conducted research at all five sites, using HUD data, baseline surveys, follow-up surveys of families, qualitative interviews, and data on juvenile crime, labor-market outcomes, and school performance. Among their findings are the following.

One to three years after the families in the experimental group moved, they lived in significantly more affluent and more racially mixed communities than families in the other two groups. In addition, those who were in the experimental group had median incomes that were 73 percent higher than the median incomes for the control group and 53 higher than the Section 8–only group. In 1997, three years after the program began, the MTO experimental group families in all five metropolitan areas lived in less-segregated neighborhoods than either of the other two groups.

Studies of adults in the experimental groups in New York and Boston reported significantly better health and emotional well-being than the Section 8–only and control groups in those cities. Mothers in both the experimental groups were much less likely to report being depressed or stressed. The parents provided more structure for their children's activities and used less restrictive parenting styles. By the third year, 10 percent fewer of the experimental group in New York City were receiving welfare. In Boston, public assistance for MTO families dropped by half, and employment in all MTO sites increased from 27 percent at the beginning of the program to 43 percent three years later. Employment in Boston increased by more than one-half.

The outcomes for children in these experimental groups were also encouraging. They attended schools that had higher pass rates, more affluent student bodies, and more resources than the schools attended by control group children. Ludwig, Duncan, and Ladd (2003) hypothesize that the peer groups in the new schools had more positive attitudes toward school than in the inner city, and this may also have contributed to good outcomes for the children.

Ludwig, Duncan, and Ladd report that young children in the experimental and Section 8–only groups "achieved higher test scores than the controls, and experienced fewer arrests for violent criminal behavior" (2003, p. 164). The authors report in some detail the assessments in Baltimore, and state that they are "largely consistent with evidence from the other MTO sites" (p. 163). Young children in the experimental and Section 8–only groups had Comprehensive Test of Basic Skills (CTBS) reading scores that were on average six to seven percentage points higher than those in the control group (i.e., in low-income urban schools). "This large effect is equal to around one-quarter of the control group mean of 25 percentile points and one-quarter of a standard deviation in the national CTBS math distribution" (p. 165). Children in the experimental group also raised their CTBS math scores about the same amount, and their pass rates on the Maryland Functional Tests' (MFT) reading test were almost double those in the inner-city schools.

High school students in the Baltimore experimental group had a more difficult transition. In the first three years of MTO, they had higher rates of grade retention, disciplinary action, and school dropout rates than the children of families in the other two groups. The authors suggest that these differences may be due to the enforcement of higher behavioral and/or educational standards in more affluent schools (Ludwig et al., 2003).

However, teens who moved from high- to low-poverty neighborhoods were arrested less often than teens in the other groups. For example, 2.7 percent of control group adolescents were arrested during an average three-month period, compared with only 1.4 percent of teens in the experimental group during the same period. Furthermore, there was a 50 percent reduction in the proportion of juveniles in the experimental group who were arrested for violent offenses. For example, in a given quarter, 3 percent of adolescents in the control group were arrested for violent crimes, compared with only 1.4 percent among the experimental group (Ludwig et al., 2003).

Research in the Boston MTO found significantly fewer behavioral and mental health problems among boys in both the experimental and Section 8-only groups, and experimental-group children were less likely to be injured or to experience asthma attacks. Among children with asthma, the number of attacks requiring medical attention fell significantly (Goering & Feins, 2003).

Additionally, the children in the experimental group in Boston were less likely to engage in antisocial behavior (Ludwig et al., 2003).

In sum, these results are in general agreement with evaluations of other mobility programs, which have generally led to "substantial improvements in . . . neighborhood conditions, physical and mental health, safety, housing conditions, adult labor-market outcomes (although the findings here are mixed)" (Johnson, Ladd, & Ludwig, 2002, p. 185) and improvements in the children's behavior and educational outcomes of families who moved.

The success of even small family supports and of a move to places of increased opportunity suggests that we should provide a financial and opportunity base for urban families. This in itself will lay the foundation for fuller child development and educational achievement.

A New Education Policy Paradigm

I have outlined a number of federal and regional polices and practices that undermine urban school quality and potential by maintaining large poverty populations in urban neighborhoods. I have also provided evidence that this poverty works against the development and achievement of urban students. Importantly, however, we also see that even modest financial and social supports for poor families enable the children to achieve at higher levels in school. This suggests that policies to counter the devastating effects of macro-economic and regional mandates and practices should "count" as policies we call on to create equity and quality in urban districts and schools.

As education policymakers and practitioners, we can acknowledge and act on the power of urban poverty, low-wage work, and housing segregation to dwarf most curricular, pedagogical, and other educational reforms. The effects of macroeconomic policies continually trump the effects of education policies.

To remove economic barriers to school quality and consequence, we can legislate a significantly higher living wage; we can create jobs in cities that offer career ladders and prepare low-income residents to fill them. And, like a number of European countries, we can tax wealthy families and corporations to pay for these and other investments. We should enforce federal antidiscrimination measures to integrate segregated housing and create public transit routes so low-income urban residents without cars are not denied access to jobs in the suburbs. Policies like these would create a social foundation on which high-quality schooling would rest. As has been the case in affluent suburbs, economic access creates the financial and political conditions in families and communities for educational commitment and reward.

In this new paradigm, education policies for which we press would take on the larger issues: Education funding reform would include the companion need for financing neighborhood jobs and decent wages. New small schools would be created as an important part of coordinated efforts at neighborhood revitalization for low-income residents. Vocational offerings in high school would link to living-wage campaigns and employers who support them. College graduation would be understood as a continuation of government's financial responsibility for public education. And lawsuits to racially integrate districts would acknowledge housing segregation as fundamental and target legal challenges accordingly.

Policies that set the standards schools must meet would identify the money, materials, teachers, courses, and neighborhood needs that must be filled in order to provide opportunities to learn at high levels. Educational accountability would be conceived as a public undertaking, centrally involving families, communities, and students, in consultation with district and government officials.

In this approach to urban school reform, "policy alignment" would not refer to the fit between education mandates issued by various levels of government and bureaucracy. The fit we would seek is between neighborhood, family, and student needs and the potential of education policies to contribute to their fulfillment.

However, economic strength and political leverage is not all that is required to transform urban education. Good schools require not only good neighborhoods, but — as equity-seeking educational reforms have promised — also the detracking of minority and working-class youth, a culture responsive to students, and assistance to teachers in their struggle to surmount the wall of resignation and defiance that separates many students from the educational enterprise.

A new paradigm of education policy is possible — one that promotes equity-seeking school change and that includes strategies to create conditions that will allow the educational improvements to take root, grow, and bear fruit in students' lives.

Notes

1. The 1958 National Defense Education Act (NDEA) funded and promoted curriculum materials, primarily in science, math, and foreign languages (e.g., the "New Math"), and some of these probably found their way into city districts and classrooms. But the NDEA was aimed at increasing the security and technological prowess of the United States, not at improving urban schools.
2. Graduation rates in large urban high schools are lower than is commonly believed. Jay P. Greene, senior fellow at the Manhattan Institute for Policy Research, calculated graduation rates in all states and large cities for major racial groups. For this calculation he first identified the eighth-grade public school enrollment for each jurisdiction and for each subgroup from the 1993 fall semester, adjusting for student movement into or out of an area. He then obtained counts of the number of regular high school diplomas awarded in the spring of 1998 when the eighth graders should have been graduating. (In calculating the 1998 graduation rate, he did not include later GED or other alternative diplomas, as the federal government does.) He found that the national graduation rate for the class of 1998 was 71 percent. For White students the rate was 78 percent, for

African American students it was 56 percent, and for Latinos, 54 percent. In fifteen of forty-five large (mostly urban) districts for which there were data, fewer than 50 percent of African American students graduated; and in twenty-one of thirty-six large, mostly urban districts for which there were data, fewer than 50 percent of Latino students graduated (Greene, 2001, pp. 1–5).

References

Anyon, J. (1979). Ideology and U.S. history textbooks. *Harvard Educational Review, 49,* 361–386.

Anyon, J. (1980). Social class and the hidden curriculum of work. *Journal of Education, 162,* 7–92.

Anyon, J. (1981). Social class and school knowledge. *Curriculum Inquiry, 11,* 3–42.

Anyon, J. (1995). Race, social class, and educational reform in an inner city school. *Teachers College Record, 97,* 69–94.

Anyon, J. (1997). *Ghetto schooling: A political economy of urban educational reform.* New York: Teachers College Press.

Anyon, J. (in press). *Radical possibilities: Public policy, urban education, and a new social movement.* New York: Routledge.

Ayres, L. (1909). *Laggards in our schools: A study of retardation and elimination in city school systems.* New York: Russell Sage.

Bernstein, J., Brocht, C., & Spade-Aguilar, M. (2000). *How much is enough? Basic family budgets for working families.* Washington, DC: Economic Policy Institute.

Bolger, K., & Patterson, C. (1995). Psychosocial adjustment among children experiencing persistent and intermittent family economic hardship. *Child Development, 66,* 1107–1129.

Bradley, R. (1984). One hundred, seventy-four children: A study of the relation between the home environment and early cognitive development in the first 5 years. In A. Gottfried (Ed.), *The home environment and early cognitive development* (pp. 5–56). Orlando, FL: Academic Press.

Brooks-Gunn, J., Duncan, G., Leventhal, T., & Aber, L. (1997). Lessons learned and future directions for research on the neighborhoods in which children live. In J. Brooks-Gunn, G. Duncan, & L. Aber (Eds.), *Neighborhood poverty, volume 1: Contexts and consequences for children* (pp. 279–298). New York: Russell Sage.

Bos, J., Huston, A. C., Duncan, G .J., Brock, T., & McLoyd, V. (1996). *New hope for people with low incomes: Two-year results of a program to reduce poverty and reform welfare.* New York: Manpower Demonstration Research Corporation.

Caspi, A., Wright, B., Moffit, E., & Silva, T. (1998). Early failure in the labor market: Childhood and adolescent predictors of unemployment in the transition to adulthood. *American Sociological Review, 63,* 424–451.

Cauthen, N., & Lu, H. (2001, August). *Living on the edge: Employment alone is not enough for America's low-income children and families* (Research Brief No. 1, Mailman School of Public Health, National Center for Children in Poverty). New York: Columbia University.

Citizens for Tax Justice. (2002). *Surge in corporate tax welfare drives corporate tax payments down to near record low.* Washington, DC: Author.

Citro, C., & Michael, R. (Eds.). (1995). *Measuring poverty: A new approach.* Washington, DC: National Academy Press.

Conley, D. (2003). *Who governs our schools? Changing roles and responsibilities.* New York: Teachers College Press.

Costello, J., Compton, S., Keeler, G., & Angold, A. (2003). Relationships between poverty and psychopathology: A natural experiment. *Journal of the American Medical Association, 290,* 2023–2029.

Cross, C. (2004). *Political education: National policy comes of age.* New York: Teachers College Press.

Dillon, S. (2003, April 30). Report finds number of black children in deep poverty rising. *New York Times*, p. 18A.

Dreier, P., Mollenkopf, J., & Swanstrom, T. (2001). *Place matters: Metropolitics for the 21st century*. Lawrence: University Press of Kansas.

Duncan, G., & Brooks-Gunn, J. (Eds.). (1997). *Consequences of growing up poor*. New York: Russell Sage.

Duncan, G., Brooks-Gunn, J., & Klebanov, P. (1994). Economic deprivation and early childhood development. *Child Development, 65*, 296–318.

Economic Policy Institute. (2002). *Economic snapshots*. Washington, DC: Author.

Economic Policy Institute. (2004). *EPI issue guide: Minimum wage*. Washington, DC: Author.

Education Trust. (2001). *The funding gap: Low-income and minority students receive fewer dollars*. Washington, DC: Author.

Entwistle, D., & Alexander, K. (1997). *Children, schools, and inequality*. Boulder, CO: Westview Press.

Fine, M. (2001, May). *Comparative analysis of the organization of high schools 1996–97, NYC Board of Education*. Findings presented at the Spencer Conference, New York. Document available at www.nysed.gov.80/emsc/docs4-99NYStrategy.ppt.3.

Galbraith, J. (1998). *Created unequal: The crisis in American pay*. New York: Free Press.

Goering, J., & Feins, J. (Eds.). (2003). *Choosing a better life? Evaluating the Moving To Opportunity social experiment*. Washington, DC: Urban Institute Press.

Greene, J. (2001). *High school graduation rates in the United States*. Washington, DC: Black Alliance for Educational Options and the Manhattan Institute.

Harrington, M. (1963). *The other America: Poverty in the United States*. Baltimore: Penguin.

Houser, R. M., Brown, B. V., & Prosser, W. R. (1998). *Indicators of children's well-being*. New York: Russell Sage.

Hout, M. (1988). More universalism, less structural mobility: The American occupational structure in the 1980s. *American Journal of Sociology, 93*, 1358–1400.

Huston, A. C., Duncan, G. J., Granger, R., Bos, J., McLoyd, V. C., Mistry, R., Crosby, D. A., Gibson, C., Magnuson, K., Romich, J., & Ventura, A. (2001). Work-based anti-poverty programs for parents can enhance the school performance and social behavior of children. *Child Development, 72*, 318–336.

Huston, A. C., Miller, C., Richburg-Hayes, L., Duncan, G. J., Eldred, C. A., Weisner, T. S., Lowe, E., McLoyd, V. C., Crosby, D. A., Ripke, M. N., & Redcross, C. (2003). *Summary report, New Hope for families and children: Five-year results of a program to reduce poverty and reform welfare*. New York: Manpower Demonstration Research Corporation.

Jackson, A., Brooks-Gunn, J., Huang, C., & Glassman, M. (2000) Single mothers in low-wage jobs: Financial strain, parenting, and preschoolers' outcomes. *Child Development 71*, 1409–1423.

Jencks, C., & Phillips, M. (1998) *The Black/White test score gap*. Washington, DC: Brookings Institution Press.

Jeremiah, L. (2003). *Family support programs and academic achievement: Lessons for Seattle*. Unpublished manuscript. Available online at http://www.evans.washington.edu/research/psclinic/pdf/02-03dp/Jeremiahdp.pdf.

Johnson, M., Ladd, H., & Ludwig, J. (2002). The benefits and costs of residential mobility programs. *Housing Studies 17*, 125–138.

Kingsley, T., & Petit, K. (2003). *Concentrated poverty? A change in course*. Neighborhood change in urban America series. Washington, DC: Urban Institute.

Klerman, L. (1991; 2003 Reprint edition). The health of poor children: Problems and programs. In A. C. Huston (Ed.), *Children and poverty: Child development and public policy* (pp. 136–157). New York: Cambridge University Press.

Korenman, S., & Miller, J. (1997). Effects of long-term poverty on physical health of children in the national longitudinal survey of youth. In G. Duncan & J. Brooks-Gunn (Eds.), *Consequences of growing up poor* (pp. 70–99). New York: Russell Sage.

Lafer, G. (2002). *The job training charade*. Ithaca, NY: Cornell University Press.

Lee, V., & Burkham, D. (2002). *Inequality at the starting gate: Social background and achievement at kindergarten entry.* Washington, DC: Economic Policy Institute.

Lu, H. (2003). *Low-income children in the United States.* New York: Columbia University, Mailman School of Public Health.

Ludwig, J., Duncan, G., & Ladd, H. (2003). The effects of moving to opportunity on children and parents in Baltimore. In J. Goering & J. Feins (Eds.), *Choosing a better life?* (pp. 153–177). Washington, DC: Urban Institute Press.

Masten, A., & Coatsworth, D. (1995). The structure and coherence of competence from childhood through adolescence. *Child Development, 66,* 1635–1659.

McLoyd, V. (1998). Socioeconomic disadvantage and child development. *American Psychologist, 53,* 185–204.

McLoyd, V., & Jartayne, T. (1994). Unemployment and work interruption among African-American single mothers: Effects on parenting and adolescent socio-emotional functioning. *Child Development, 65,* 562–589.

Miao, J., & Haney, W. (2004). High school graduation rates: Alternative methods and implications. *Education Policy Analysis Archives, 12*(55). Available online at http://epaa.asu.edu/epaa/v12n55.

Michaloupolos, C., Tattri, D., Miller, C., Robins, P. K., Morris, P., Gyarmati, D., Redcross, C., Foley, K., & Ford, R. (2002). *Making work pay: Final report on the self-sufficiency project for long-term welfare recipients.* New York: Manpower Demonstration Research Corporation.

Mishel, L., Bernstein, J., & Boushey, H. (2003). *The state of working America: 2002/2003.* Ithaca, NY: Cornell University Press.

Mishel, L., Bernstein, J., & Schmitt, J. (2001). *The state of working America: 2000/2001.* Ithaca, NY: Cornell University Press.

Morris, P., Huston, A.C., Duncan, G.J., Crosby, D., & Bos, J. (2001). *How welfare and work policies affect children: A synthesis of research.* Washington, DC: Manpower Demonstration Research Corporation.

O'Connor, A. (2003, October 21). Rise in income improves children's behavior. *New York Times,* p. F5.

Odden, A., & Picus, L. (1992). *School finance: A policy perspective.* New York: McGraw-Hill.

Orfield, M. (2002). *American metropolitics: The new suburban reality.* Washington, DC: Brookings Institute.

Phillips, K. (2002). *Wealth and democracy: A political history of the American rich.* New York: Broadway Books.

Phillips, M., Brooks-Gunn, J., Duncan, G., Klevanov, P., & Crane, J. (1998). Family background, parenting practices, and the Black/White test score gap. In C. Jencks & M. Phillips (Eds.), *The Black/White test score gap* (pp. 103–145). Washington, DC: Brookings Institution Press.

Phillips, M., Crouse, J., & Ralph, J. (1998). Does the Black/White test score gap widen after children enter school? In C. Jencks & M. Phillips (Eds.), *The Black/White test score gap* (pp. 229–272). Washington, DC: Brookings Institution Press.

Ravitch, D. (2000). *The great school wars: A history of the New York City public schools.* Baltimore: Johns Hopkins University Press.

Rubinowitz, L., & Rosenbaum, J. (2002). *Crossing the class and color line: From public housing to White suburbia.* Chicago: University of Chicago Press.

Rusk, D. (1999). *Inside game/outside game: Winning strategies for saving urban America.* Washington, DC: Brookings Institution.

Sampson, R., Morenoff, J., & Gannon-Rowley, T. (2002). Assessing "neighborhood effects:" Social processes and new directions in research. *Annual Review of Sociology, 28,* 443–478.

Seitz, V., Rosenbaum L., & Apfel, N. (1985). Effects of family support intervention: A ten-year follow-up. *Child Development 56,* 376–391.

Short, K., Iceland, J., & Garner, T. (1999). *Experimental poverty measures: 1998.* Washington, DC: U.S. Census Bureau.

Smith, J., Brooks-Gunn, J., and Klebanov, P. (1997). Consequences of living in poverty for young children's cognitive and verbal ability and early school achievement. In G. Duncan & J. Brooks-Gunn (Eds.), *Consequencs of growing up poor* (pp. 132–189). New York: Russell Sage Foundation.

Stein, S. (2004). *The culture of educational policy.* New York: Teachers College Press.

Stipic, D., & Ryan, R. (1997). Economically disadvantaged preschoolers: Ready to learn but further to go. *Developmental Psychology, 33,* 711–723.

Sugland, B., Zaslow, M., & Brooks-Gunn, J. (1995). The early childhood HOME inventory and HOME short form in differing socio-cultural groups: Are there differences in underlying structure, internal consistency of subcases, and patterns of prediction? *Journal of Family Issues, 16,* 632–663.

Tyack, D. (1974). *The one best system: A history of American urban education.* Cambridge, MA: Harvard University Press.

White, K. (1982). The relationship between socioeconomic status and academic achievement. *Psychological Bulletin, 91,* 46–81.

Wrigley, J. (1982). *Class politics and public schools: Chicago 1900–1950.* New Brunswick, NJ: Rutgers University Press.

I would like to thank my colleague Tony Picciano for his thoughts.

Comparative and International Education: A Journey toward Equality and Equity

NELLY P. STROMQUIST
University of Southern California

Comparative and international education is a field characterized by wide and constant borrowing of theories, concepts, and research methods from the social sciences. While some see this multidisciplinarity as cause for alarm, others consider it a source of intellectual wealth. Given the multiple disciplines, perspectives, and events that attract the attention of comparative and international education (CIE hereafter), it is difficult to present a consensual view of contributions, progress, and challenges to date. In examining the trajectory of CIE over several decades, I lean on my professional experience, a review of the major journals in the field, and my five years as associate editor for the *Comparative Education Review*. Even so, I make no claims that my account is the most complete or most accurate. Since education systems are intended to have positive effects on society both by providing essential skills and by promoting social mobility and inclusion of all citizens, this review focuses on the issues of equality and equity in the comparative education context.

In 1969, two distinct groups of professionals joined to form the Comparative and International Education Society. In general, comparative education emphasizes the understanding of the dynamics of educational change and seeks to detect patterns of change across countries. International education concentrates primarily on developing countries and endeavors to gear education to the improvement and building of nation-states. CIE is found in university courses and programs and in academic journals, as well as in negotiations between and within states for purposes of policymaking. The ideas and preferences of CIE professionals are played out in various spaces: economists prevail in government and international transactions; in universities, there is a more balanced array of sociologists, political scientists, and, increasingly, anthropol-

Harvard Educational Review Vol. 75 No. 1 Spring 2005

ogists; in civil society — particularly nongovernmental organizations (NGOs), trade unions, and religious groups — one finds adult educators.

In our recent history, the world has witnessed a second world war, the enactment of the UN Universal Declaration of Human Rights (1948), pervasive conflict along political ideologies in the Cold War, and the formal demise of colonialism. It has also seen several conventions in favor of political, economic, and social rights (particularly the 1979 Convention on the Elimination of All Forms of Discrimination Against Women and the 1989 Convention on the Rights of the Child); numerous global agreements on issues ranging from gender equality to protection of the environment; and increasing tensions along economic and religious lines. During those decades, CIE professionals have shifted their views and priorities, moving from strong reliance on the power of education to shape society and promote development to recognition that education is one force among many — one that is sometimes exploited politically to promise more than it can deliver. In the 1960s, themes included modernization, development, and social transformation; by the 1980s, concerns were more circumscribed, emphasizing basic needs, income generation, and employment (Kelly, 1987). Salient CIE themes at the beginning of the twenty-first century include globalization, gender in education, education in development, and equality in education (Cook, Hite, & Epstein, 2004).

CIE for Prediction or for Understanding?

In the early days of comparative education — the 1960s — there was a firm expectation that the field would develop its own research tools and theories in order to identify regularities characterizing educational systems in the world. Inspired by the significant methodological contributions of the social sciences during World War II, comparative educators such as Bereday (1964) and Noah and Eckstein (1968) guided the quest toward laws governing educational systems. At the same time there were those, notably Holmes (1965) and King (1968), who were less certain about finding regularities through decontextualized and ahistorical knowledge of education. Today the latter perspective is more prevalent, as it is now considered fruitless to search for a general theory of education to explain change and persistence, although it is recognized that conflict is always present in educational decisions and even processes (Behrman, 2003; Bray, 2003; Carnoy & Samoff, 1990; Farrell, 1988).

In the 1960s and 1970s, the Ford Foundation provided support to several American universities to create international education programs. This support played a decisive role in incorporating the social sciences in the design of curricula for educational programs and financed the training of a large cadre of American and international graduate students as comparative educators. Over time, CIE has shifted from a predominantly equilibrium/functionalist paradigm (based on assumptions of widespread social consensus) to more emphasis on neo-Marxist/conflict theoretical frameworks (more attentive to questions of power differences and domination). According to Crossley and Jarvis (2000), CIE now increasingly recognizes the cultural dimension of education, particularly its efforts to understand distinctions and similarities between cultures in the western and eastern parts of the world. Models focusing on modernization, world systems, and globalization are in common usage, while critical sociological, postmodernist, and feminist paradigms are increasingly present. The field continues to give limited attention to historical and philosophical aspects of education, and to the interaction between education and mass media.

At present, international comparisons coexist with within-nation studies. Large-scale, cross-national studies are expensive and tend to be limited in number, the best known being those conducted by the International Association for the Evaluation of Educational Achievement (IEA) and by the Organization for Economic Cooperation and Development (OECD). A review of publications in three major CIE journals over forty years (Rust, Soumare, Pescador, & Shibuya, 1999) found that fewer than one-third of the articles were based on research designs that explicitly compared two or more countries. Two main foci have characterized comparative studies. Some have focused on student performance, and others have sought to explain the functioning and impact of education systems.

Student Achievement Studies

From 1967 to 2004, IEA had conducted more than twenty cross-national studies focusing on school curricula. The rich information collected in the national studies and the background information gathered for each student benefited the study of educational policy in the context of overall social and economic policy (Husen, 1987). In addition, their multivariate analysis enabled education researchers to disentangle larger social influences and home background from factors operating in the school. The IEA studies have contributed powerful conceptualizations of the education system, covering not only a wide range of inputs and important outcomes, but also making us aware of promising elements in the processes of teaching and learning. IEA studies introduced the distinction between the official, the implemented, and the attained curriculum, a framework that permeates all IEA studies.

Given the complex nature of the learning experience, the quantitative studies provide limited explanation for variation in individual achievement. The Six-Subject Survey (1970), which employed over 500 independent variables, accounted for only 45 percent of the between-student variance for any one school population in a country. Some differences, however, have been detected between developed and developing countries. Major determinants of student achievement in developing countries include the availability of trained teachers, books, and basic infrastructure, such as electricity and water (Velez, Schiefelbein, & Valenzuela, 1993). According to Cronbach (as cited in Riddell, 1989), the majority of studies of educational achievement have produced "false conclusions" because of the "misapplication of a single-level model to a reality that is clearly hierarchical" (p. 484).

In recent years, a new set of quantitative studies has emerged, of which the best known are the Programme for International Student Assessment (PISA) investigations organized by OECD. These studies follow conceptualizations of school impact similar to those used by IEA, but differ in their data collection and analysis. IEA uses intact classrooms, and thus analyzes data by grade, whereas PISA gathers and analyzes data by student age. Moreover, PISA studies do not engage in multilevel analysis of schooling effects.

Recent cross-national studies have incorporated a greater number of countries, including developing countries. Their findings in general show that students from developed countries do much better than those from developing countries; students in urban areas have higher achievement than those in rural regions; and those in private schools perform better than those in public schools (see, e.g., PASEC, 2002; PIRLS, 2001; PISA, 2000, 2003; TIMS, 1995; TIMSS-R, 1999). These findings confirm what one would expect, and perhaps reflect the substantial differences in public investment across countries, in the education and economic conditions of teachers, and in school infrastructure within countries. Few studies compare educational achievement between countries within specific developing regions. In one of the few studies of particular interest, Casassus, Froemel, Palafox, and Cusato (1998) compared thirteen Latin American countries in primary school language and mathematics achievement. The researchers found that Cuba surpassed all other countries in both subjects by between 1.5 and 2 standard deviations. Explanations for this extraordinary performance have not been investigated; Silvestre (2004) argues that the synergistic array of particular conditions in Cuban society, including health, housing, and sustained educational investments, account for the results.

Critical Theory Studies

In stark contrast to cross-national quantitative surveys of student achievement, critical theory studies employ qualitative approaches attentive to history and to cultural and political transactions. Bourdieu and Passeron's work (translated into English in 1977) on cultural reproduction and the role of the school in legitimating the dominant cultural capital has helped to present schooling as a terrain far from neutral to all social groups. The extension of Bourdieu's thought by Bowles and Gintis (1976) to the economic reproduction function of schooling further created awareness of the way schools work. Their "correspondence theory" argued that the hierarchically structured patterns of values, norms, and skills that characterized the workforce and the dynamics of class interaction under capitalism were mirrored in the dynamics of daily classroom transactions.

Critical theoreticians such as Gramsci, Freire, and Habermas have shaped the debate of international and comparative education. Gramsci (1992,

1994), exploring the efficacy of persuasion over coercion and the role of education in the establishment of a hegemonic view, has helped us understand the persistence of subordinate social groups in all areas of society. Gramsci's work brought to CIE important, accessible concepts such as hegemony and counterhegemony, the "organic intellectual," and a revitalized civil society. Freire is another important contributor, whose writings were first introduced to North American audiences in the *Harvard Educational Review* in 1970. His *Pedagogy of the Oppressed*, first published in 1970, has sold more than 750,000 copies worldwide and is one of the most broadly read books in education. Freire's work underscores the political nature of education and calls for processes, notably "conscientization" — a deliberate examination of our economic and political environment — as a prerequisite to envisaging how knowledge can serve to eliminate oppression and create a just society. The Frankfurt School further unveiled traditional power relationships and the ideology that supported them by highlighting the importance of cultural and literacy forms in the creation of social representations. Habermas (1984), the contemporary heir of the Frankfurt School, reinforced the emancipatory potential of dialogue inherent in communicative action while defending the value of modernity and reason.

More directly linked to schooling, work by Willis (1977) represented a turning point in the development of resistance theories, which explained how individuals confronted their oppression and how they sometimes ended up reproducing what they sought to question. Subsequent work by Giroux (1983) questioned reproduction theory for downplaying the importance of human agency and resistance, and argued instead that schools are "contested terrains" marked not only by structural and ideological contradictions but also by collective student resistance. From Giroux (1989) we have learned that pockets of resistance in schools can serve as models for new forms of learning and social relations, and that efforts toward democracy can take place in and through teachers who act as transformative intellectuals. These teachers engage in activities such as discussing collective struggles "in which suffering was shaped and contested" and identifying "the material and ideological preconditions" that must be in place to create effective schools (pp. 99, 101).

Dependency theory, which maintains that the development of industrialized countries is predicated on the exploitation of the less developed regions of the world, was first applied in Latin America to explain developing countries' failure to attain the economic growth that modernity promised. This theory was first applied to CIE by Carnoy in 1974. The extension of dependency to education focused on the exportation of cultural models from industrialized countries to the periphery, showing that what was promoted by hegemonic countries' national systems did not often favor the particular needs and situations of the Third World. Altbach and Kelly's (1984) analysis of education in former colonized countries was among the first to document the existence of differentiated educational systems within a country. Their research found that in former colonies there were two distinct education systems, both controlled by the colonizing country and aimed at different populations.

CIE has seen frequent attacks on modernity, a notion largely taken for granted under both functionalist and conflict paradigms. Disappointed by the unfulfilled promise of industrialization, urbanization, and economic growth, several social scientists — including such CIE researchers as Rust (1991), Masemann and Welch (1997), and Paulston (1999) — have moved toward the explanatory frameworks afforded by postmodernity, neocolonial theories, and poststructuralism. CIE researchers have borrowed heavily from Foucault; his discussions of the symbiosis between power and knowledge (1977), the transactional nature of power and its manifestations at multiple levels (1980) have been invaluable to analyses of education among subordinated groups.

The Role of Education

Over the years, CIE has seen drastic shifts in the definition of "national development," from an emphasis on economic growth to a concern for redistribution of assets and opportunity, with implications for the diminution of inequalities, including poverty. Freire (1970) introduced a modified view of development that embraced material and spiritual dimensions in which he defined education as the practice of freedom. Sen (1999) further expanded the definition of development by including the notion of "capabilities," specifically, what individuals are able to do in areas that are essential to improving the quality of their lives. Economic analyses of the contribution of education, which was deemed consequently essential to the formation of human capital (Schultz, 1961, 1970), propelled attention to the field. Harbison and Myers' 1964 economic study, based on seventy-four countries, supported the conclusion that human resources were an essential ingredient to modernization. A study of sociopsychological variables in six developing countries led Inkeles and Smith (1974) to conclude that schooling is the most powerful factor in making individuals modern (which the two authors defined as people who favor rationality, are open to new experiences, defy superstition, and assume control of their lives through planning), and that education was a more powerful tool to develop modern attitudes than were work in modern industrial factories and the mass media.

From 1945 to 1981, 105 new states joined the United Nations. The independence of African countries spurred attention to education expansion, leading to studies that sought to explain how educational systems function and expand. Work by Archer (1979), focusing on European systems, found that structural characteristics (centralized vs. decentralized) generated different dynamics in the form and pace of educational change. Collins (1979) found that mass education resulted from competition among status groups for social dominance. Others, including Boli, Ramirez, and Meyer (1985), contended that global diffusion of democratic values is at work and that the gradual adoption of these values creates modern polities that reflect collective religious, political, and economic preferences.

Following World War II, many hoped that educational institutions would create economic growth and good citizenship, but subsequent disappointments led to more modest assessments of the potential of education. This was captured by Weiler (1978), who argued that the field had moved from the age of innocence to the age of skepticism. Today, the lack of correlation between educational levels and economic growth in some regions of the world, particularly Latin America and Africa, reveals the critical importance of factors other than education in economic and social development. Moreover, the lack of correlation between income distribution and educational levels suggests that formal schooling — which has become increasingly segmented by social class — is not fostering the empathy and respect for the "other" that is necessary for a fair social contract.

Equality/Diversity

Equality of opportunity is generally considered one of the most enduring educational issues. It is at the heart of the notion of education as a means for mobility in societies that consider themselves meritocratic. The first shock about the conditions of a disadvantaged group came with Myrdal's (1944) study on the "American dilemma." This report underscored the contradictions between a country's professed commitment to human rights and the oppression of Black people. Myrdal's recognition of "white supremacy" ignited new understanding and gave strength to studies of racism and schooling not only in the United States, but also in the rest of the world, particularly South Africa and several Latin American countries with indigenous populations. The U.S. Supreme Court's desegregation decision in *Brown v. Board of Education of Topeka, Kansas* (1954) opened wide debate over education in both industrialized and developing countries.

The 1966 Coleman Report in the United States and the 1967 Plowden Report in the United Kingdom investigated students' achievement across different schools. Both reports showed the salience of family conditions in successful student learning, but found that schools also did contribute to cognitive gains. About the same time, Illich (1971) issued his debate-provoking challenge to "deschool" society, rejecting the claim that education behaved as a "great equalizer" and asserting instead that it served to manipulate individuals into a highly consumerist society. *Harvard Educational Review* produced a special issue on equal educational opportunity in 1968. In it, Coleman (1968) addressed the complexities inherent in the definition of educational equality, ranging from differences in inputs, processes, and racial composition of schools, to differences in outcomes for individuals of equal and unequal backgrounds.

Substantial differences still exist in understanding the causes of educational (and social) inequalities and therefore in the nature of the solution. At one end we have educators and politicians who envision a within-the-school set of changes, including better trained teachers, more and better educational materials, and adequate infrastructure. At the other end we have many social scientists who think that solving inequality necessitates interventions in society as a whole, including areas of health, employment, and housing. The two proposals are not mutually exclusive; in practice, however, most measures to combat inequality have concentrated on schools and have been piecemeal.

International education has seen the implementation of a number of compensatory and remedial measures in the industrialized world. Ethnic minorities in the United States — who exhibit the greatest incidence of poverty — have benefited from compensatory education programs. With increased immigration, ethnic segregation in schooling has also emerged in Europe. In response, countries such as the U.K., France, Belgium, and the Netherlands have set up compensatory educational programs, though the teaching support and the additional materials provided by these programs have not been able to erase the disadvantages suffered by minority children. Consequently, this part of the world has seen a shift toward other interventions: preschool and early school education, greater reliance on school-community and school-parent relations, promotion of integrated services, and an emphasis on the transition from school to work (Driessen, 2001).

In developing countries, where disadvantages are even stronger for the poor and minorities, few interventions have been enacted. While the disparities in educational achievement and attainment between urban and rural areas are sizable, practically no developing country has a rural public policy. Two programs exceptions are PROGRESA (now called *Oportunidades*) in Mexico, which seeks to provide rural children with nutrition, health, and education stipends, and the District Primary Education program in India, which prioritizes scheduled castes and scheduled tribes (legally classified and protected groups of disadvantaged people) and supplies them with resources to improve student access and retention, teacher training, and instructional aids. Neither program has been able to affect student achievement but they have increased enrollment and retention.

Another way of serving the disadvantaged has been through the provision of school content that recognizes their cultural identity and teaches non-U.S. minorities to respect the "other." Multicultural education is considered an offshoot of the civil rights movement. It developed in the United States and the U.K. as a government response to the increasing number of people from minority cultures (Banks, Banks, & Banks, 1989), and spread to the European Community in the 1980s. It continues to take two different approaches: One concentrates on the acceptance and tolerance of cultural diversity, the other questions cultural assumptions and stereotypes and locates them in a terrain shaped by asymmetric power relations. This second approach calls for antiracist, antisexist, and other antidiscriminatory perspectives in education; not surprisingly, this approach is applied much less frequently than the first.

Multicultural education has had its detractors, including those who hold that teaching minority cultures strengthens prejudice, separatism, and even racism (Schlesinger, 1992). In countries with sizable ethnic populations, such as Guatemala, Bolivia, and Peru, the need for "multicultural" and "intercultural" education (the latter term implying greater two-way communication between cultures) is recognized, but adequate programs do not exist. Bilingual and intercultural education reflect the very political nature of education. What emerges in reality are not tangible struggles between ethnic groups and government, but "unresolved" issues regarding teaching in native languages or the comprehensive training of teachers to address the characteristics and needs of diverse student populations. There is a dearth of studies that focus on the school experiences of children of subordinate social classes and ethnicities.

Gender in Education

The 1970s' women's movement triggered analyses of schools and classrooms that examined the role of teachers' expectations and practices in the creation of masculinity and femininity norms, and the type of knowledge provided by formal education. The women's movement, and the gender and feminist theories that followed, also brought a more sober look into what seemed to be an end in itself: access to schooling. With the adoption of the concept of gender in the 1980s, studies have been more sensitive to the construction of gender ideologies and practices affecting women and men simultaneously, although asymmetrically. Many works have influenced the understanding of gender in international education. Salient among them is Connell's work (1987) showing the intertwined nature of gender, power, and politics. Empirical and conceptual work by Pateman (1988), Kelly and Elliott (1982), Arnot and Weiler (1993), Blackmore and Kenway (1993), Weiner and Arnot (1987), and Stromquist (1991) demonstrated the gendered nature of the state and its social institutions, documented the myriad ways the formal and hidden curricula shaped women's conceptions of self, and advanced the debate toward a critical feminist approach.

Significant reference to women in CIE can be detected as early as 1979, when the *Harvard Educational Review* produced a special issue on women and education. Other special issues appeared in the *Comparative Education Review* in 1982 (and later in 2004) and *Comparative Education* in 1987. The understanding of women's education has moved from a focus on gender differences to describing difficult conditions experienced by female students, to identifying the variables that accounted for differential access and attainment (years of schooling) between boys and girls, and most recently to documenting the patterns and causes of masculinity in schools. Legislation such as the Civil Rights Act of 1964 and Title IX of the Higher Education Amendments of 1972 — both in the United States — expanded the definition of women's rights in education. Notable among them was the removal of discrimination in access to higher education programs, scholarships, employment, and sports, and the redefinition of sexual harassment as sexual discrimination.

Current gender studies are now more aware of the impact of culture, the state, the labor market, and the family on educational outcomes of women and men at all levels of education. Because research on gender issues is poorly funded, limited cross-national studies exist on this crucial topic. The most common type of study has been content analysis of textbooks. Many have documented the tendency of textbooks to present women in biased ways, primarily as mothers, homemakers, and caregivers, with limited roles as professionals. Textbooks and curricular content have improved in several countries, both developed and developing. However, it is still the case that references to women decline as grades become more advanced and that women's professional roles are presented in narrower ranges than those of men. Pre- and in-service training of teachers in gender issues remains sporadic and reaches only a small minority of teachers. Currently, in the midst of the HIV-AIDS epidemic, many sex education programs in developing countries present sexual relations as sinful and dangerous and thus advise abstinence, despite the fact that sexual behavior is increasingly prevalent among adolescents. In countries with high mortality rates in general, almost 40 percent of the deaths among females between the ages of fifteen and twenty-nine are due to this epidemic; another 20 percent of female deaths are due to maternal conditions (pregnancy and delivery complications, and abortions; Lloyd, 2005). Since HIV/AIDS affects youths in great proportions and kills both parents and teachers, it unleashes challenges for what schools should do for new generations of students.

Most policymakers, including the Vatican, would accept today that women's education is important. But there are still some who believe that what is needed is simply that women accommodate to family and outside work by becoming professionals while continuing to engage in domestic management. It is insidious to maintain that professional women can be successful while completely absorbing family care and related duties. Tead (1947) noted that there was an increasing number of women in higher education in the United States but added that the "psychological and social success of the home requires that each college woman will assume her share and take her part in local civic affairs, to the infinite toning up of the quality of health, recreation, art, education, and worship of her community" (p. 160). More than fifty-five years later, the Vatican similarly welcomed women's higher levels of education while denying that sex differences are "mere effects of historical and cultural conditioning" and observing that there is an "irreplaceable role of women in all aspects of family and social life involving human relationships and caring for others" (Vatican, 2004). The educational system's inability to question ideologies of women's and men's work and the gendered power relations in the private sphere exists across all levels of education, from primary to tertiary education.

A number of studies in industrialized countries have found that schools and classrooms are very much involved in producing masculinity and femininity through teacher practices and attitudes, and various forms of peer transactions (Connell, 1995; Mac an Ghaill, 1994). Such studies are much less frequent in developing countries, but the few that exist indicate a similar pattern. In recent IEA and PISA studies, researchers have noticed a slight superiority of girls in reading achievement. There are no studies that explain why girls are doing better than boys in reading, while they continue to perform less well in math and science. A possible and partial explanation might be that in societies where women are delegated to domestic spheres, reading may be a source of vicarious living. The stagnation of boys' enrollment in sub-Saharan African countries and the weaker performance of boys in reading in the international comparisons has prompted claims by governments and some donor agencies that the women's movement has gone "too far" and that efforts must be taken to help male students.

As reflection on gender and education has progressed, it has revealed a clear intersection of gender with other forms of social disadvantage, such as class, ethnicity, and race. A challenge to both research and policy at present is how to address this persistent confluence of social markers. Yet it is evident that girls' enrollment and attainment rates on aggregate are increasing faster than those of boys (Lloyd, 2005). There is no solid explanation for this, since governments have not engaged in policies focusing on the situation of girls, except for a handful of countries in Africa. The reasons might lie elsewhere: more educated parents who seek more schooling for all their children, smaller families that diminish the need for child care, and increasing urbanization that brings schools into greater proximity and facilitates access to domestic technologies.

Before 1980 the field did not closely investigate women, family, or the relationships among education, health, and nutrition. Today, however, we realize that it would be incomplete to carry out an educational analysis if it did not acknowledge the differential experiences and consequences of schooling for men and women. We have gained considerable understanding of both the reproductive and transformative possibilities of schooling. In international development, there has been a transition from a women-in-development focus (WID) to a gender-and-development framework (GAD). Unfortunately, the educational initiatives under GAD, although stronger in conceptual argumentation, have remained weak and fragmented in terms of societal interventions to modify gender relations.

Nonformal Education and Informal Learning

While it has been common knowledge that learning occurs in venues beyond schooling, Coombs and Ahmed (1974) brought the concept of nonformal education to CIE. This concept was accompanied by a more systematic look at the potential of alternative forms of education for youths and adults to provide useful knowledge and training outside the strictures of formal educational systems and without leading to formal degrees.

Nonformal education — defined as that offered primarily to youth and adults outside the strictures and conventions of formal schooling, such as workshops on family nutrition or in union organizing (Coombs & Ahmed, 1974) — is still far from being accepted as having equal value to formal education. Some educational researchers (e.g., Bock & Papagiannis, 1983) see it as technical and vocational education that creates second-class citizens. Other researchers, particularly in Latin America (Arnove, 1994; Schugurensky, 2003; Torres, 1990), see education for adults outside the school as providing critical learning about one's society, including knowledge of a contested nature. This approach, often called popular education, received substantial support in the ideas of Gramsci, Freire, and liberation theology. Gramsci's (1992, 1994) notion of "the organic intellectual" brought new understanding to the role of adult educator. His notion of education as political and politics as essentially educational also helped revolutionize previously technocratic and instrumental views of adult education. Freire's (1970) questioning of "banking education," which concentrates on conveying information to individuals rather than incorporating their experience and prior knowledge in their learning process, and the need for ongoing dialogue through cultural circles also modified pedagogical practices with adults.

Foley (1999, 2004) has contributed significantly to adult education. Using the concept of informal learning, he has transformed the old concept of political socialization to focus on the learning that occurs through struggle and transformative action. Informal learning — that which occurs through engagement in various political and cultural actions — is helping individuals, both men and women, to acquire knowledge and skills through participation in organizations that seek change or that question changes that have been made without the people's consent.

Adult illiteracy in the world has diminished in percentages but has remained rather stable in absolute numbers. Two-thirds of illiterates are women, a proportion that has proven extremely tenacious. The large number of youth and adult illiterates — estimated to be close to 900 million people — constitute a population that can be served only through nonformal education. UNESCO, the international body in charge of education, has been found to foster forms of adult education that offer remedial rather than transformative literacy (Jones, 1990). Few countries give sufficient attention to the condition of rural education; in fact, it is difficult to identify a country today that has a rural education policy.

Much popular education work (the version of nonformal education in many developing countries) has been carried out by NGOs and community-based organizations, which are small groups that function informally at the neighborhood level. Popular education practices and philosophies prevail in many parts of the developing world. For example, South Africans benefited greatly from this mode of education in their struggle against apartheid. Adult education today, in its traditional and popular education forms, is still not properly acknowledged by CIE, in either research or academic training. Much of the existing literature on the subject is in languages other than English and is not published in academic journals.

Globalization and Its Impact

Through scholarly work, journalistic accounts, and recent events, the concept of globalization has pierced our consciousness in indelible ways. Northern scholars and institutions — those located in the industrialized countries — perceive globalization primarily as a set of technological discoveries that have compressed time and space, leading to the integration of economies and societies through flows of goods, finance, information, and labor. From the perspective of southern scholars and activists — those inhabiting the less developed regions of the world — globalization has economic and political features that perpetuate and even exacerbate disadvantages faced by less industrialized countries.

Tikly (2001) and other northern scholars assert that cultural hybridization is leading to new individual and group identities. Other accounts, particularly outside education, present a different picture, one in which political forces continue to shape the world but have taken on new forms. Robinson (2004), working with the notion of the transnational state (TNS), which he conceives as "a particular constellation of class forces and relations bound up with capitalist globalization" (p. 100), holds that this apparatus is multilayered and multicentered. The TNS is said to link institutions informally but effectively with distinct gradations of "state-ness." These supranational organizations are economic and political, formal and informal. The economic forms include the International Monetary Fund, the World Bank, the World Trade Organization (WTO), and the regional development banks. The political forms include the Group of Eight, OECD, the European Union, the United Nations, the Association of Southeast Asian Nations, the North American Free Trade Agreement, and others.

Today, 300 transnational companies own one-fourth of the productive assets of the world (Korten, 2001). In shaping the nature of the economy, these transnational organizations and firms introduce new demands and roles for education. While contemporary society is portrayed as the "knowledge society" — and it is evident that people with higher levels of education command higher salaries and standard of living — it is also clear that the economic system produces individuals who will occupy the lower ranks. This dynamic requires an education system that favors competition and inculcates among "losers" the notion that merit alone determines life chances.

As society has become globalized, there have been substantial changes in postsecondary education. This portion of the education sector has expanded greatly, through both conventional (based on physical student and teacher presence) forms of education and distance (particularly Internet-based) education. As more individuals earn technical, vocational, and professional degrees, society gains greater amounts of information and knowledge. Yet, the expansion of postsecondary education has occurred through great doses of diversification, in this case the sprouting of numerous institutions of varied quality and social recognition. Governance under a competitive ethos is changing the university toward a managerial and entrepreneurial organization, as documented by Slaughter and Leslie's (1997) comparative study. Similar changes are being reported in universities throughout the developing world. Altbach (1987) highlighted the crucial role of higher education, which he termed "the most important intellectual institution with widespread impact on culture, politics, and ideology" (p. 2). Much for-profit expansion of universities is occurring through distance education. While there were large open universities in Indonesia and Thailand before the presence of globalizing forces, English-speaking universities from the United Kingdom, the United States, Australia, New Zealand, and India have now entered the education market, creating possibilities for democratization as well as social exclusion that are not fully understood. Orfield (1992), reviewing ten years of policy debate in the United States (1980–1989), found that the research shows "a direct relationship between income and college attendance and that higher tuition produces declining participation" (p. 362). Today, with the increasing impact of economic and technological globalization on postsecondary education access, curricula, objectives, governance, and the changing structure of the labor market and economy in general, higher education has become a crucial topic for CIE study.

Many feminists (Blackmore, 2000; Kenway & Kelly, 2000; Stromquist, 2002) find that with globalization we are experiencing the reconfiguration of all forms of oppression. Since globalization is characterized by an uneven distribution of power, it is far from certain that the reality of globalization matches the "global citizenship" discourse, by which a transnational sense of purpose and obligation is developing. Interdependency characterized by denser relations in politics, economics, communications, and the environment is emerging, but it is less evident that transnationalism — defined as a position that seeks the common good and thus the reduction of all types of inequality across nation-states — may prevail. Vilas (2004) holds that a global capitalism — one without nationality and without ties to states, territories, and national markets — lacks empirical validity.

New Educational Actors

In recent decades, abetted by globalization forces, significant players other than nation-states have emerged. On the one hand, international finance agencies and transnational organizations are assuming greater presence and power than ever before in educational decisionmaking circles. On the other hand, NGOs are attaining greater responsibilities in the provision of education.

Financial and Transnational Institutions

The World Bank (WB) attained visibility in CIE with its 1980 *Education Policy Paper*, which some of its staff called "a modern Bible on educational development" (Psacharopoulos, 1981, p. 141). Since then, other reports have followed, notably *Education in Sub-Saharan Africa* (1988), *Higher Education: The Lessons of Experience* (1994), and *Priorities and Strategies in Education* (1995). Typically, WB policy papers and reports present a strong defense of formal schooling, arguing that the human capital developed by schooling not only alleviates poverty but also contributes to growth in national productivity and income. WB research focuses on identifying what works in education and skirts any discussion of political and economic issues affecting equality and equity in education, except perhaps for its recent consideration of corruption as a development issue. Similar positions and reports have been produced by the Inter-American, the Asian, and the African Development banks, regional banks with significant influence of their own.

The WB gives priority to education issues dealing with efficiency, equality, accountability, decentralization, user fees, privatization, and related forms of parental choice. The efficiency orientation in WB policy, however, usually boils down to privatization as a means to avoid what is seen as inherent waste in low student retention, low achievement, and high dropout rates due to the monopoly held by public schools. Equality is often mentioned, yet the clearest treatment by the WB is its recommendation that the middle and upper social classes pay for their own higher education. Psacharopoulos (see, e.g., 1986) suggested using incentives to create private schools and to provide credits/loans so that people could invest in education. His perspective is quite prescient in WB literature and programs. A WB publication that has had a significant impact in developing countries is *Improving Primary Education in Developing Countries* by Lockheed and Verspoor (1991). The WB's position that the economic situation in Africa had deteriorated due to shortages of educated manpower or deficiencies in educational quality has been questioned by CIE scholars, notably Foster (1998), who maintains that although there are inefficiencies in its educational systems, the region is substantially more affected by the depressed commodity prices and the heavy interest burden on its external debts.

The World Bank prefers to conduct its own research, which is almost exclusively quantitative. With more than 1,200 researchers on staff, the WB has become a major actor in education, influencing policies in both developing countries and former communist countries. Bilateral agencies, even those that defend more humanistic development models, generally defer to WB positions.

Two other organizations that have a major impact on educational decisions in the international arena are the OECD and the United Nations Development Program (UNDP). The OECD is notable for its various studies focusing on student achievement, while the UNDP garners much attention for its annual *Human Development Report*. The report has introduced two indices that are frequently used by various educational ministries and agencies: the Human Development Index (in existence since 1990 and available for 162 countries by 2001) and the Gender Empowerment Measure (since 1995), both of which consider levels of education and literacy rates. These indices have provided metrics that enable countries to track their performance over time and to do so in comparison with similar nations. UNDP now also produces reports for specific countries.

Social Movements

Social movements crystallized in the form of NGOs have multiplied in recent decades as a response to economic and social hardships invoking numerous issues: access to land, gender equality, apartheid, privatization of basic services, domestic violence, HIV/AIDS, neoliberal policies, hunger, and others. NGOs' work in education takes two forms: 1) a type of adult education that tends to be both critical of the status quo and proactive, and thus focused on social transformation, particularly gender and ethnic change, and 2) a more incipient but rapidly expanding form that seeks to provide formal schooling to rural children who are not being served by government schools, mainly in sub-Saharan Africa and South Asia.

Successful examples from the U.S. civil rights movement, women's rights movements, and ecological movements throughout the world have provided constant inspiration and support to progressive NGOs. Many of the educational programs, especially those centered on women's advancement, work to empower participants, something not attempted by most formal education programs (Stromquist, in press).

CIE research does not cover this very important set of actors. For instance, it is not following to any significant degree the educational role of social movements involving indigenous people, particularly in Latin America, where strong networks are developing the capacity to convene regional conferences. These groups are examining themes such as autonomy and territory, diversity and plurinationality, rights of people and nations, militarization (a reference to current events to fight the drug traffic in the Amazon), and the role of women in the construction of a plurinational state.

Public Policies in Education

Two different models of public policy are used to characterize nations: the socialist egalitarian model in communist countries and the liberal competitive model in capitalist countries. Today we see a movement toward convergence, with the liberal capitalist model prevailing, in which schools are organized for competition — trying to outperform one another in student performance — rather than equity. Developing countries now tend to invest little in education, as large proportions of the national budgets are allocated to pay the external debt (UNDP, 1999). Ironically, at a moment of state retrenchment, official discourse related to government policies abounds. We know relatively little about policy formulation and subsequent implementation in developing countries. Many governments subscribe to global agreements to expand the educational supply and quality but then do little to reach those objectives. One explanation might be the essentially distributive nature of educational policy, a process that seldom requires a significant redistribution of wealth and thus does not threaten powerful domestic groups. Most policy analyses concentrate on the policy itself and give limited consideration to the historical and political context in which the policy functions. An exception to this is the work by Carnoy and Samoff (1990) that produced a state-centered political perspective in its comparative study of national systems of education. Hannum's (1999) work on China has also been of interest because of its identification of radical changes in educational policies, even within a socialist regime.

Many educational policies today resemble one another. Innovations frequently involve decentralization, accountability, parental choice, and privatization. This convergence appears for several reasons, including the fast spread of information and thus the "contagion effect," and the powerful leverage wielded by multilateral and bilateral aid agencies. Developing countries' need for additional resources through loans or grants makes them vulnerable to the technical advice of these agencies; consequently, "external players seek to shape the policy-related judgments and decisions made within the normal operation of decision-making in sovereign states" (Jones, 1990, p. 43). The diffusion of policies has also been explained by the fact that supranational organizations are staffed by transnational functionaries who work with their transnational counterparts in the transformed national states (Robinson, 2004).

Two major global policies have affected education since 1990. The Education for All (EFA) policies endorsed by most national governments seek to ensure access to basic education for all, reduce gender disparities at all levels of education, and eliminate illiteracy. The Millennium Development Goals, unanimously agreed upon by the United Nations in 2000, were in part an attempt to rescue the EFA goals and set the year 2015 as their ultimate attainment date. Though widely accepted, few national education plans have so far designed interventions to meet these goals, much less allocated resources to specific ends.

Increasingly, accountability policies mandate testing to determine how schools are performing and how quality could be elevated. In an article entitled "Testomania," Sorokin (1955), one of the greatest sociologists of his time, questioned the scientific nature of tests, calling them "a new form of the old beliefs in revealing omens, paper-pen magical operations, or vocal incanta-tions dressed in modern scientific garb" (p. 213). Contemporary critics main-tain that testing now functions as an instrument that reflects the cultural capi-tal students possess before coming to school and registers the value added by the school only in modest ways. Test scores are usually reported by school, with little statistical control for differences in inputs and student background, which perpetuates a belief in the beneficial results of the private school and the "low quality" of public schools. Experts on the production of tests have re-marked that test items designed to guide the teaching/learning process require different features from those designed to compare schools.

Decentralization policies are widespread. They range from the state level to the municipal level to the school level. Decentralization offers the promise of release from the bureaucratic and financial control of central ministries, and the possibility of adapting curricula to meet local cultures and needs. How-ever, when enacted, these policies have been characterized by the simple transfer of miniscule budgets to local levels, along with a lack of training for these new administrative responsibilities. This leaves decentralization suscep-tible to failure. Although no studies have been conducted to date on the im-pact of decentralization on equality, there is reason to believe that the subor-dination of women and ethnic groups may not be ameliorated through decentralization, as antagonisms and authoritarian practices are sometimes stronger at the community level than at national levels.

In recent years we have seen intensified debate on schools as quasi-markets: public financing to ensure that all have access to basic education, private fi-nancing to ensure free school choice. The UN Universal Declaration of Hu-man Rights enacted in 1948 (Article 26) declares education a basic human right and recognizes the obligation of the state to provide free and compul-sory elementary education. It also gives parents "a prior right to choose the kind of education that shall be given to their children," a right reiterated in the International Covenant on Economic, Social, and Cultural Rights (1966). Arguments favoring the creation of charter schools and the use of school vouchers that ensure the transfer of public funding primarily to private insti-tutions originated in the United States in 1955. They received attention in the developing world in the 1990s, primarily due to endorsement by the World Bank. However, there has been only limited adoption of the voucher model, primarily because it requires a complex system of administration and monitor-ing. Society faces a serious dilemma. Parental choice is part of essential free-dom. Yet, in selecting private schools for their children, parents — especially those who have greater levels of income and wealth — contribute to what has become an unstoppable phenomenon: the segmentation of the educational system into the public and private. Given the persistent criticism of public schools, privatization is gaining favor among parents who seek to provide their children a more competitive position in society and the economy.

Recent consideration of public policies highlights the need to move into second-generation reforms to make the structural reforms that have existed since the late 1980s effective. Unlike those in the past, the new measures would not avoid public regulation but would instead pursue "sensible legislation" so that government will function efficiently and engage in clear rules for taxation, adjudication of service, electoral reforms, and changes in tariff structures to complement unskilled labor (Naím, 1994; Navia & Velasco, 2003). What constitutes a major analytical contribution of second-generation reforms is the sober realization that they offer low political visibility and are not appealing to politicians seeking short-terms results. These reforms are also likely to counter the interests of highly organized and vocal groups, ranging from teachers and judicial unions to the upper echelons of public bureaucracy, state and local governments, owners and managers of private monopolies, and the medical establishment. However, the heterogeneity of these groups may provide space for maneuvering and negotiating common agreements.

Conclusions

In its path toward equality, CIE has seen a few watershed moments, most of which have come from outside education in the form of judicial decisions, social movements, or neoliberal policies imposed by international institutions. Some events have accelerated the consideration of equality and its attainment, particularly for women. Others are broadening the separation between social classes and reducing the possibilities of good quality public education schooling for ethnic and rural populations.

CIE theories and research methods have developed greater precision and complexity over time. However, the influence of CIE is determined not only by its intellectual value but also by the proximity of its practitioners to the circles of power. Those wielding influence are not academics but rather the staff members of international organizations and their transnational counterparts who subscribe to dominant, market-oriented development models that are not substantiated by empirical research.

Are educational systems in developing countries improving over time? Pertinent cross-national comparisons are relatively recent. They show that students in developing countries attain much lower scores than those in the industrialized nations. It is also clear, however, that public investment in education in developing countries tends to be low. Are minorities doing better today than in earlier decades? Their educational access has been expanding, but primary school completion rates and learning achievement remain low. Studies from Mexico, Brazil, and India show that ethnic minorities and castes have not been able to significantly improve their disadvantaged status in educational attainment. Are women registering improved access and performance compared to men? By and large they are, even in sub-Saharan African countries where educational access has stagnated in the last decade. However, attitudes about gender have changed only marginally, as the women/motherhood nexus prevails. According to UNDP statistics, people live longer, healthier lives, are more educated, and have higher incomes than thirty years ago (2001). This is true on the *aggregate*, but the world is becoming polarized by region, by social class, and by rural/urban residence, with the income gap between the richest 10 percent and the poorest 10 percent of most countries increasing in most instances.

Our future looms imperfect and with enormous challenges. We face three distinct paths: 1) to witness and document the progressive privatization of education and the parallel deterioration of its public counterpart with no particular value judgment; 2) to respond through greater research on the impact of current state retrenchment on equality and equity policies and educational rights, while asserting a position vis-à-vis the emerging reality; or 3) to go beyond research and establish alliances among academics, progressive educators, and activists of all generations to shape an educational world responsive to justice and solidarity. What will we choose? Comparative educators cannot remain indifferent to growing global inequalities in the economy, political power, and education. We must respond through collective action and span diverse communities within and between the north and south. The path of exclusive engagement in research activities will only contribute to CIE's decline.

References

Altbach, P. (1987). *Higher education in the Third World: Themes and variations.* New York: Advent Books.

Altbach, P., & Kelly, G. (Eds.). (1984). *Education and the colonial experience.* New Brunswick, NJ: Transaction Books.

Archer, M. (1979). *Social origins of educational systems.* London: Sage.

Arnot, M., & Weiler, K. (Eds.). (1993). *Feminism and social justice in education: International perspectives.* London: Falmer Press.

Arnove, R. (1994). *Education as contested terrain: Nicaragua, 1979–1993.* Boulder, CO: Westview.

Banks, J., Banks, C., & Banks, M. (Eds.). (1989). *Multicultural education: Issues and perspectives.* Boston: Allyn & Bacon.

Behrman, E. (2003). The political economy of educational reform in Australia, England and Wales, and the United States. In R. Arnove & C. Torres (Eds.), *Comparative education: The dialectic of the global and the local* (2nd ed., pp. 252–291). Lanham, MD: Rowman & Littlefield.

Bereday, G. (1964). *Comparative methods in education.* New York: Holt, Rinehart and Winston.

Blackmore, J. (2000). "Hanging onto the edge": An Australian case study of women, universities, and globalization. In N. Stromquist & K. Monkman (Eds.), *Globalization and education: Integration and contestation across cultures* (pp. 333–352). Lanham, MD: Rowman & Littlefield.

Blackmore, J., & Kenway, J. (Eds.). (1993). *Gender matters in educational administration and policy: A feminist introduction.* London: Falmer Press.

Bock, J., & Papagiannis, G. (1983). *Nonformal education and national development: A critical assessment of policy, research, and practice*. New York: Praeger.

Boli, J., Ramirez, F., & Meyer, J. (1985). Explaining the origins and expansion of mass education. *Comparative Education Review, 29*, 145–170.

Bourdieu, P. & Passeron, J. C. (1977). *Reproduction in education, society and culture*. London: Sage.

Bowles, S., & Gintis, H. (1976). *Schooling in capitalist America: Educational reform and the contradictions of economic life*. New York: Basic Books.

Bray, M. (2003). Control of education: Issues and tensions in centralization and decentralization. In R. Arnove & C. Torres (Eds.), *Comparative education: The dialectic of the global and the local* (2nd ed., pp. 204–228). Lanham, MD: Rowman & Littlefield.

Carnoy, M. (1974). *Education as cultural imperialism*. New York: D. McKay.

Carnoy, M., & Samoff, J. (Eds.). (1990). *Education and social transformation in the Third World*. Princeton, NJ: Princeton University Press.

Casassus, J., Froemel, J. E., Palafox, J. C., & Cusato, S. (1998). *Primer estudio internacional comparativo sobre lenguaje, matemáticas y factores asociados en tercer y cuarto grado*. Santiago, Chile: Oficina Regional de Educacion para America Latina y El Caribe.

Coleman, J. S. (1968). The concept of equality of educational opportunity. *Harvard Educational Review, 38*, 7–22.

Collins, R. (1979). *The credential society: A historical sociology of education and stratification*. New York: Academic Press.

Connell, R. (1987). *Gender and power: Society, the person and sexual politics*. Sydney, Australia: Allen & Unwin.

Connell, R. (1995). *Masculinities: Knowledge, power and social change*. Cambridge, Eng.: Polity Press.

Cook, B., Hite, S., & Epstein, E. (2004). Discerning trends, contours, and boundaries in comparative education: A survey of comparativists and their literature. *Comparative Education Review, 48*, 123–149.

Coombs, P., with Ahmed, M. (1974). *Attacking rural poverty: How nonformal education can help*. Baltimore: Johns Hopkins University Press.

Crossley, M., & Jarvis, P. (Eds.). (2000). Comparative education for the twenty-first century [Special issue]. *Comparative Education, 36*(3).

Driessen, G. (2001). The limits of educational policy and practice? The case of ethnic minorities in The Netherlands. *Comparative Education, 36*, 7–20.

Farrell, J. (1988). *The national unified school in Allende's Chile*. Vancouver: University of British Columbia Press.

Foley, G. (1999). *Learning in social action: A contribution to understanding informal education*. London: ZED.

Foley, G. (Ed.). (2004). *Dimensions of adult learning: Adult education and training in a global era*. Maidenhead, Eng.: Open University Press.

Foster, P. (1989). Some hard choices to be made. *Comparative Education Review, 33*, 104–110.

Foucault, M. (1977). *Discipline and punish*. London: Tavistock.

Foucault, M. (1980). *Power/knowledge: Selected interviews and other writings, 1972–1977*. New York: Pantheon.

Freire, P. (1970). *Pedagogy of the oppressed*. New York: Herder and Herder.

Giroux, H. (1983). *Theory and resistance in education: A pedagogy for the opposition*. Exeter, NH: Heinemann.

Giroux, H. (1989). *Schooling for democracy: Critical pedagogy in the modern age*. New York: Routledge.

Gramsci, A. (1992). *Prison notebooks*. New York: Columbia University Press.

Gramsci, A. (1994). *Letters from prison*. New York: Columbia University Press.

Habermas, J. (1984). *The theory of communicative action*. Boston: Beacon Press.

Hannum, E. (1999). Political change and the urban-rural gap in basic education in China, 1949–1990. *Comparative Education Review, 43*, 193–211.

Harbison, F., & Myers, C. (1964). *Education, manpower, and economic growth: Strategies of human resource development.* New York: McGraw-Hill.

Holmes, B. (1965). *Problems in education: A comparative approach.* London: Routledge & Kegan Paul.

Husen, T. (1987). Policy impact of IEA research. *Comparative Education Review, 31,* 29–46.

Illich, I. (1971). *Deschooling society.* New York: Harrow Books.

Inkeles, A., & Smith, D. (1974). *Becoming modern: Individual change in six developing countries.* Cambridge, MA: Harvard University Press.

Jones, P. (1990). UNESCO and the politics of global literacy. *Comparative Education Review, 34,* 41–60.

Kelly, G. (1987). Comparative education and the problem of change: An agenda for the 1980s. *Comparative Education Review, 31,* 477–489.

Kelly, G., & Elliott, C. (Eds.). (1982). *Women's education in the third world. Comparative perspectives.* Albany: State University of New York Press.

Kenway, J., & Kelly, P. (2000) Local/global labor markets and the restructuring of gender, schooling, and work. In N. Stromquist & K. Monkman (Eds.), *Globalization and education: Integration and contestation across cultures* (pp. 173–195). Lanham, MD: Rowman & Littlefield.

King, E. (1968). *Comparative studies and educational decisions.* Indianapolis: Bobbs-Merrill.

Korten, D. (2001). *When corporations rule the world* (2nd ed.). Bloomfield, CT: Kumarian Press.

Lloyd, C. (Ed.). (2005). *Growing up global: Transitions to adulthood in developing countries.* Washington, DC: National Academy Press.

Lockheed, M., & Verspoor, A. (1991). *Improving primary education in developing countries.* New York: Oxford University Press.

Mac an Ghaill, M. (1994). *The making of men: Masculinities, sexualities and schooling.* Buckingham, Eng.: Open University Press.

Masemann, V., & Welch, A. (1997). *Tradition, modernity and postmodernity in comparative education.* Amsterdam: Kluwer.

Myrdal, G. (1944). *An American dilemma: The Negro problem and modern democracy.* New York: Harper & Row.

Naím, M. (1994). Latin America: The second stage of reform. *Journal of Democracy, 5,* 32–48.

Navia, P., & Velasco, A. (2003). The politics of "second-generation reforms." In P.-P. Kuczynski & J. Williamson (Eds.), *After the Washington consensus: Restarting growth and reform in Latin America* (pp. 265–303). Washington, DC: Institute for International Economics.

Noah, H., & Eckstein, M. (1968). *Toward a science of comparative education.* New York: Macmillan.

Orfield. G. (1992). Money, equity, and college access, *Harvard Educational Review, 62,* 337–372.

Pateman, C. (1988). *The sexual contract.* Stanford, CA: Stanford University Press.

Paulston, R. (1999). Mapping comparative education after postmodernity. *Comparative Education Review, 43,* 438–463.

Psacharopoulos, G. (1981). The World Bank in the world of education: Some policy changes and some remnants. *Comparative Education Review, 17,* 141–146.

Psacharopoulos, G. (1986). The planning of education: Where do we stand? *Comparative Education Review, 30,* 560–573.

Riddell, A. (1989). An alternative approach to the study of school effectiveness in Third World countries. *Comparative Education Review, 33,* 481–497.

Robinson, W. (2004). *A theory of global capitalism: Production, class, and state in a transnational world.* Baltimore: Johns Hopkins University Press.

Rust, V. (1991). Postmodernism and its comparative education implications. *Comparative Education Review, 35,* 610–626.

Rust, V., Soumaré, A., Pescador, O., & Shibuya, M. (1999). Research strategies in comparative education. *Comparative Education Review, 43,* 86–109.

Schlesinger, A. M. J. (1992). *The disuniting of America*. New York: Norton.

Schugurensky, D. (2003). Two decades of neoliberalism in Latin America: Implications for adult education. In S. Ball, G. Fischman, & S. Gvirtz (Eds.), *Crisis and hope: The educational hopscotch of Latin America*. New York: RoutledgeFalmer.

Schultz, T. (1961). Investment in human capital. *American Economic Review, 1,* 1–17.

Schultz, T. (1970). *Investment in human capital: The role of education and of research*. New York: Free Press.

Sen, A. (1999). *Development as freedom*. New York: Knoff.

Silvestre, M. (2004). El LLECE y Cuba. Retrieved May 6, 2004, from Comunidad Educativa@gruposyahoo.com.arg.

Slaughter, S., & Leslie, L. (1997). *Academic capitalism: Politics, policies, and the entrepreneurial university*. Baltimore: Johns Hopkins University Press.

Sorokin, P. (1955). Testomania. *Harvard Educational Review, 25,* 199–213.

Stromquist, N. (Ed.). (1991). *Women and education in Latin America*. Boulder: CO: Lynne Rienner.

Stromquist, N. (2002). *Education in a globalized world: The connectivity of economic power, technology, and knowledge*. Lanham, MD: Rowman & Littlefield.

Stromquist, N. (in press). *Organizaciones feministas y la transformación social en América Latina*. Lima: Ediciones Flora Tristan/Manuela Ramos.

Tead, O. (1947). Women's higher education — past, present, and future. *Harvard Educational Review, 18,* 151–161.

Tikly, L. (2001). Globalisation and education in the postcolonial world: Towards a conceptual framework. *Comparative Education, 37,* 151–171.

Torres, C. (1990). *The politics of nonformal education in Latin America*. New York: Praeger.

United Nations Development Programme. (1999). *Human development report*. New York: Author.

Vatican. (2004). *Letter to bishops of the Catholic church on the collaboration of men and women in church and in the world*. Rome: Vatican. Retrieved July 2, 2004, from http://www.vaticanva/roman_curia/congregations/cfaith/documents.

Velez, E., Schiefelbein, E., & Valenzuela, J. (1993). *Factors affecting achievement in primary school: A review of the literature for Latin America and the Caribbean*. Washington, DC: World Bank, Human Resources Division.

Vilas, C. (2004). *Entre la desigualdad y la globalización: La calidad de nuestras democracias*. Retrieved September 9, 2004, from http://www.universidadabierta.edu.mx/SerEst/MCP/Processos%Electorales%20III_archive.

Weiler, H. (1978). Education and development: From the age of innocence to the age of scepticism, *Comparative Education, 14,* 179–198.

Weiner, G., & Arnot, M. (1987). *Gender under scrutiny: New inquiries in education*. London: Open University Press.

Willis, P. (1977). *Learning to labour: How working class kids get working class jobs*. Farnborough, Eng.: Saxon House.

World Bank. (1988). *Education in sub-Saharan Africa: Policies for adjustment, revitalization and expansion*. Washington, DC: Author.

World Bank. (1994). *Higher education: The lessons of experience*. Washington, DC: Author.

World Bank. (1995). *Priorities and strategies for education: A World Bank review*. Washington, DC: Author.

Afterword

KEVIN K. KUMASHIRO
Center for Anti-Oppressive Education

A few years ago, I attended a symposium on Asian/Pacific American (APA) studies at which a student asked how the field attended to diversity within Asian/Pacific America along the lines not only of ethnicity, but also gender, social class, religion, and so forth. One of the leading scholars in the field responded that attention to its own margins was central to APA studies. APA studies, like other ethnic studies, originated as a response to the dominance of a certain group and their perspective in society, namely, White Americans. That commitment to amplifying voices from the margins and interrupting the status quo has expanded and continues to expand to other dimensions of diversity among APAs. This means that, paradoxically, a field that examines and challenges the marginalizing of APAs expects that it will also marginalize APAs, albeit in different ways, and therefore needs to make challenges to its oppressive tendencies a central part of its work.

Some might find quite disconcerting this notion that anti-oppressive activism is paradoxical. Saying who we are and what we are fighting for entails saying who we are not and what we are not fighting for, which is why even when we work against inequity and injustice, we cannot help but to allow some inequities and injustices to persist unchallenged. Anti-oppressive work is necessarily partial, making it necessary for us to be diligent in reflecting on and interrupting the unintended outcomes of whatever we do and however we do it. Perhaps not surprising, attending to its own margins, as in any field, has been a challenge for APA studies since its beginnings. Nonetheless, I find the goal quite inspiring because it provides an idealized model for me to imagine how to engage in my own research and activism on schooling.

Of course, I am not alone. The retrospectives in this volume describe significant strands of research over the past seventy-five years that have highlighted, examined, contested, and advanced issues of equity and diversity in education. At once discouraging and hopeful, the various authors highlight recurring barriers and promising movements toward social justice in education. This leads me to ask, How do we foster the development of new research and

Harvard Educational Review Vol. 75 No. 1 Spring 2005

new researchers to build on these promises? In concluding this volume by asking questions that push the field ever further, I will (re)read the chapters with specific attention to the paradox mentioned above.

A First Reading: Troubling Foundations

I read all the chapters with much appreciation for the informative overviews of the various disciplines of research in education. Especially helpful was the attention paid to the histories of contestation within each of these disciplines over the topics, methods, and even purposes that "should" define each one. That is, in addition to various debates over what constitutes the proper object and method of inquiry for researchers in a given discipline were debates over why the discipline existed in the first place and what effect — direct or indirect, macro or micro — it was to have. This means not only asking how better to do what we already do in our field; it also means asking whether we should significantly rethink why we do what we do.

The authors continue this tradition by raising provocative questions about what is often taken for granted in the various disciplines of educational research, especially regarding the proper topics, methods, and purposes of research. They not only reveal ways that the foundations of our disciplines are troubling or partial, but also engage in troubling or raising critical questions about the very notion of a foundation to the disciplines. Such questions suggest that the "foundations" of the various disciplines may themselves operate paradoxically when working toward social justice.

Ellen Condliffe Lagemann makes just such an argument about prevailing assumptions about research. U.S. federal policies currently privilege only certain forms of research in education, namely, those that fit what some have defined as "scientific." While some researchers have responded by raising awareness of ways that marginalized forms of research can be both valid and valuable, other researchers have responded by conforming to such standards in order to compete for funding and publishing. Similar pressures have historically characterized the field of research on the history of education when debating and then privileging only certain views of what should be researched, and how, and with what outcome. Lagemann responds with perspective and vision to suggest that different traditions of research — the traditions that arise from "science," as narrowly defined, as well as the traditions that arise from the humanities — can lead to different insights and implications for change. What would perhaps be a better evaluation of research than its conformity to one form of science is its usefulness in improving schools today.

Kieran Egan focuses on a different arena of educational research by urging a troubling of prevailing assumptions about learning. Tracing the influence of such canonical thinkers as Spencer and Piaget on how educators think about the cognitive development of youth, Egan argues that some concepts have become so taken for granted as to be unquestioned in much of the history of educational psychology and its framing of how children learn, how they should learn, or how they best learn. There are multiple ways of conceptualizing how students learn, each with its own strengths and weaknesses, and yet few have taken the bold and urgently needed step of critically examining the partial consequences of dominant conceptualizations. Answering this charge, Egan examines not only the logical inconsistencies of some of these concepts, but also their impact on how groups of students are unjustly categorized, differentiated, and marginalized.

Sonia Nieto urges a troubling of prevailing assumptions about teaching. Throughout the twentieth century and especially in recent decades, researchers have offered competing and overlapping explanations for the differential levels of achievement between groups of students, especially groups based on race. Nieto lucidly outlines these various cultural, structural, and interpersonal explanations, as well as the suggestions for methods of classroom instruction that address them. She reminds us that teaching must be envisioned with attention to the context in which it occurs. This includes not only the demographic context and the ways that different forms of teaching can disadvantage or marginalize some groups of students. This also includes the political context and ways that the best of intentions in individual classrooms can be thwarted by policies or politics that undo moves toward greater equity, access, and awareness, including moves toward desegregation and bilingual and multicultural education. To improve teaching, educators must address the social and political contexts that can help and hinder that process.

Jean Anyon extends Nieto's analysis in her call for an expansion of what makes for educational policy. With compelling detail, Anyon describes the ways that social and economic policies can exacerbate poverty and, in turn, the strong connection between poverty and academic underachievement (or, conversely, between increased financial resources in the family and raised academic achievement for the student). While many may acknowledge these links, research and advocacy on educational policy continue to focus on changing schools without also changing the socioeconomic structures of the communities in which those schools operate. Without attention to economic policy, students from poorer communities remain disadvantaged and marginalized. Anyon urges researchers and advocates to create economic policy (for the community/societal context of schools) as part of educational policy, or to risk initiating reforms that continue to have limited impact.

Nelly Stromquist makes a parallel call for an expansion of what makes for comparative and international education (CIE) research. Significant shifts characterize the history of research on CIE, especially from the search for general themes about schooling across contexts to the search for explanations of inequities along specific lines of race, culture, gender, and other markers. Looking outward with breadth and insight, Stromquist notes that in this age of globalization and postcolonialism, the factors that come to bear on schooling in a given nation and that disadvantage some groups of students are unlikely limited to the institutions and socioeconomic structures within that nation. Thus, Stromquist urges that more attention be paid to other agents, including international governing and economic bodies, when examining the relationships and possible fissures between schooling and social stratification.

Each of the disciplines of educational research illustrates the paradox of addressing some forms of inequity and injustice even while complying with, contributing to, or even creating other forms. By asking us to critically examine the foundations of our disciplines — to acknowledge the partialities and attend to the margins — the authors suggest new and innovative directions for educational research that, while uncomfortable and uncertain, promise to take us further toward social justice.

A Second Reading: Troubling Initiations

Admittedly, there are many ways to synthesize the field of educational research. The *Harvard Educational Review* has a long history of publishing on issues of equity and diversity, and following this tradition, the editors of this volume invited authors to contribute retrospectives that attended to these issues. I believe their chapters have much promise for pushing the field of educational research toward greater social justice. But I also believe that much stands in the way of doing such research, and perhaps more importantly, of preparing and enabling researchers to do so.

Asking troubling questions about the foundations of any discipline requires contesting the terrain created by those who came before. This may be difficult when being mentored or evaluated by those who helped to create those foundations. Emerging scholars may have difficulty proposing feminist critiques of histories of education if their mentors wrote some of those histories. Emerging scholars may have difficulty proposing critical readings of race in urban reforms if their mentors advocate for such reforms. Emerging scholars may have difficulty proposing analyses of heterosexism in ethnic studies if their mentors lead such studies. And, indeed, when meeting with graduate students of color, one of the concerns I hear most often is the resistance they encounter when trying to approach their research in ways that not only depart from, but also raise troubling questions about, the work of their mentors. This resistance is similarly encountered when presenting at conferences or submitting manuscripts to peer-reviewed journals. Rather than inviting and enabling researchers to continue the tradition of troubling the very foundations of educational research, leading researchers — including leaders on issues of equity, diversity, and social justice — sometimes resist such movement, as when they say that such research is not credible because it fails to ask the right questions.

The contributors to this volume suggest one reason for this resistance: Becoming a researcher in a discipline often involves learning to think disciplinarily, that is, learning to think as others have thought before. Such initiation helps to mold the identities or practices that are shared, and thus are constitutive or distinguishing of a field. But in doing so, such initiation also requires a conformity to or repetition of topics, methods, and purposes of research that often go unquestioned, perhaps because they are posited as the cornerstones of a given discipline. What this means is, initiation often involves learning *not* to question certain foundations of whatever discipline into which we are being initiated.

In this way, we can see parallels between disciplinary advancement and identity-based activism. As noted earlier, activism around any given identity — Asian/Pacific American, prolabor, feminist, queer — involves first defining who we are and what we are fighting for, which cannot be done without also defining who we are not and what we are not fighting for. Given the multiple axes of diversity and the shifting dynamics of privilege within any group, such definitions cannot help but operate paradoxically, creating margins within the very groups that were created as sources of empowerment. Such inherent limitations and paradoxes of identity politics require that activists always look to their own margins and ask troubling questions about how practices intended to interrupt some inequities and injustices might unintentionally contribute to other inequities and injustices.

Unfortunately, after initiation, it seems that some researchers become so invested in their own ideas that they resist the challenges necessary to advance the field. They become the leaders, the experts on how things are or what works best. This is perhaps not surprising, since the academy places value on those researchers who build the foundations of their disciplines and pressures other researchers to follow suit. From getting published and funded to establishing tenure and reputation, researchers often become leaders in a field because they advance a theory that becomes a cornerstone of a discipline, often forgetting that they got there because they, too, had to trouble what came before them.

The field of educational research continues to exhibit formidable barriers to anti-oppressive change. The experience of emerging scholars of color with resistance and marginalization is but one small indication. But change is happening, led in no small part by this journal.

With Praise and Hope

The *Harvard Educational Review* has become one of the flagship journals in the field of educational research. With its articles frequently discussed in courses and cited in other research publications, *HER* helps to define what counts as the cutting edge of educational research. Increasingly over the past few decades, the *Harvard Educational Review* has showcased research with topics and methods that attend to diversity and advance equity in new and innovative ways. I find it all the more reassuring that such an institutionalized venue as the *Harvard Educational Review* is being led, and has been led for decades, by some of the brightest and most progressive voices from the margins, namely, students. We need more opportunities for voices from the margins to help trouble our disciplines and push our field further toward social justice. I have little doubt that *HER*'s current and future editors and contributors will continue to bring progressive research to bear on educational policy and practice, and I look forward to seeing the changes that result.

Notes on Contributors

JEAN ANYON is a professor of social and educational policy at the Graduate Center, City University of New York, where she also directs the education policy strand of the doctoral program in urban education. Her research centers on the intersection of race, class, and education. Anyon's work includes some of the most oft-cited pieces in the field and has been reprinted in more than forty collected volumes. Her publications include *And We Are Not Yet Saved: Social Policy, Urban Education, and a New Civil Rights Movement* (2005), *Ghetto Schooling: A Political Economy of Urban Educational Reform* (1997), and *Social Class and the Hidden Curriculum of Work* (1980). For nearly a decade, Anyon taught elementary school in Brooklyn, Philadelphia, and Washington, DC.

KIERAN EGAN is a professor of education at Simon Fraser University in British Columbia, Canada. He is one of the leading thinkers on the development of cognition in children. He is the author of numerous books and scholarly papers on topics ranging from the role of imagination in teaching to the historical development of developmental theories. His recent publications include *An Imaginative Approach to Teaching* (2005) and *The Educated Mind* (1997); the latter has been translated into numerous languages. Egan began his career in education as a high school teacher in Warwick, England, before coming to the United States to pursue doctoral work at Stanford and Cornell.

KEVIN K. KUMASHIRO, a former teacher and teacher educator, is the founding director of the Center for Anti-Oppressive Education and a senior program specialist in human and civil rights at the National Education Association. He is author of several books on anti-oppressive education, including *Troubling Education* (2002), for which he received the 2003 Myers Outstanding Book Award, and *Against Common Sense: Teaching and Learning toward Social Justice* (2004).

ELLEN CONDLIFFE LAGEMANN is the dean of the Harvard Graduate School of Education and the Charles Warren Professor of the History of American Education. A leading historian of education with particular expertise in education research, Lagemann is the author or editor of nine books, as well as numerous articles, reviews, and book chapters. Some of her recent publications include *An Elusive Science: The Troubling History of Education Research* (2000), *Issues in Education Research: Problems and Possibilities* (with L. Shulman, 1999), and *Philanthropic Foundations: New Scholarship, New Possibilities* (1998). Formerly president of the Chicago-based Spencer Foundation, Lagemann was also a professor at New York University, where she served as founding chair of the Department of the Humanities and the Social Sciences and director of the Center for the Study of American Culture and Education in the School of Education. Before joining the faculty at NYU, Lagemann taught for sixteen years at Teachers College and was also a member of the Department of History at Columbia.

SONIA NIETO is a professor of education at the University of Massachusetts Amherst. Her research focuses on multicultural education, teacher education, and the education of Latinos, immigrants, and other students of culturally and linguistically diverse backgrounds. She serves on several national advisory boards that focus on educational equity and social justice, and has received numerous awards for her advocacy and activism. Her books include *Affirming Diversity: The Sociopolitical Context of Multicultural Education* (4th ed, 2004), *What Keeps Teachers Going?* (2003), and *The Light in Their Eyes: Creating Multicultural Learning Communities* (1999), and two edited books, *Why We Teach* (2005) and *Puerto Rican Students in U.S. Schools* (2000).

GARY ORFIELD is professor of education and social policy at the Harvard Graduate School of Education, where his work is centered around the study of civil rights, education policy, urban policy, and minority opportunity. He is cofounder and director of The Civil Rights Project at Harvard University, an initiative that is developing and publishing a new generation of research on multiracial civil rights issues. Orfield has participated as an expert witness in several dozen civil rights cases, including the University of Michigan Supreme Court case that upheld the policy of affirmative action in 2003. Orfield's many publications include two recent edited volumes, *Dropouts in America: Confronting the Graduation Rate Crisis* (2004) and *Racial Inequity in Special Education* (with D. Losen) (2002), both from Harvard Education Press.

NELLY P. STROMQUIST is a professor at the University of Southern California's Rossier School of Education. She specializes in issues related to international development, education, and gender, which she analyzes from a critical sociological perspective. Stromquist has considerable experience in formal and nonformal education, particularly in Latin America and West Africa. She is the author of numerous articles and books, including *Education in a Globalized World: The Connectivity of Economic Power, Technology, and Knowledge* (2002) and *Literacy for Citizenship: Gender and Grassroots Dynamics in Brazil* (1997). She is editor of *Women in the Third World: An Encyclopedia of Contemporary Issues* (1998).

Personal Statements
from Contributors

As part of this commemorative collection, the authors were invited to describe their relationship with the *Harvard Educational Review* and the role the journal has played in their professional careers. In this section, contributors share these reflections as both readers and authors of the journal.

Gary Orfield

In reflecting on the history of the *Harvard Educational Review,* I think it is appropriate to recognize the contributions of the *Review* and its editors. The *Harvard Educational Review* has, of course, published a number of the most influential articles on education in this era. In my years at the Harvard Graduate School of Education (HGSE), I have known many of the students who served on the Editorial Board, heard occasional complaints about something they decided to publish, and often been fascinated by the originality of ideas and viewpoints they fostered. I think that it has been very healthy for our field to have an important journal run by students who take their task very seriously and work much harder than many editorial boards I know. It is not accidental that they have a much larger readership than most academic journals. Their particular advantage is that they represent a generation ahead of the curve of educational practice, and throughout my experience at HGSE, the Board has maintained the kind of serious diversity that I believe enriches the ideas of the journal and gives it something of a critical edge in educational research and policy discussions.

Ellen Condliffe Lagemann

I am pleased that the editors of the *Harvard Educational Review* have decided to devote their seventy-fifth anniversary volume to matters pertaining to education research. *HER* has the largest circulation of any journal in education, and many seminal articles have appeared in its pages. I have been a reader of *HER* for more than twenty-five years, and during that period *HER* has published many classic and controversial articles. In my view, the *HER* has been at its best when it focuses on current controversies in the field. Given the present interest in education research, I expect that this commemorative volume will be one of the best.

Kieran Egan

The *Harvard Educational Review* first became known to me when I came from England to do doctoral studies at Stanford. Needing to become oriented to the strange culture of education in North America, I plunged — or perhaps tripped — in alarm and amazement into the array of journals available in the campus libraries. *HER* seemed particularly helpful in that it usually offered a mix of articles, some of which exposed the dominant social concerns that education sought to address, while others offered incisive views of important theoretical issues. It seemed, better than any other journal, a good index to what education meant in America during those years, and has continued to do so since.

SONIA NIETO

"Strategies for Failure" by Annie Stein (1971) was the first article I ever read in the *Harvard Educational Review*. Addressing the institutional structures that produced failure in the New York City Public Schools, the article spoke to me as both a student in the very same school system and, later, as a young teacher in it as well. Not only was it riveting to read, but it also forever changed how I was to view education and teaching. Several years later, as a doctoral student, I came across two previously published articles: Joan and Steven Baratz's hard-hitting and compelling "Early Childhood Intervention: The Social Science Base of Institutional Racism" (1970), where I saw the words "institutional racism" in a scholarly piece for the first time; and Arthur Jensen's notorious "How Much Can We Boost I.Q. and Scholastic Achievement?" (1969). In this article, Jensen, an apologist for scientific racism, argued that there was an inherent difference in the intelligence of Blacks and Whites, and it left me angry and disheartened about the future of public education. These articles represent the wide range of research brought to light in the *Harvard Educational Review*. Whether we have agreed with everything in its pages or not, in the seventy-five years of its existence, *HER* has published thought-provoking, cutting-edge articles that challenge readers to reflect, talk back, and change their ideas and their practice. I have been honored to be part of the *Harvard Educational Review* through a number of articles I have written over the years, and I am honored to be part of this momentous commemorative issue.

JEAN ANYON

It was 1976 and I was completing my doctoral thesis in psycholinguistics — comparing the language acquisition theories of Jean Piaget and Noam Chomsky. Dissatisfied with what I considered the apolitical nature of cognitive psychology, I began reading education scholarship on the side, and came across Bowles and Gintis's newly published *Schooling in Capitalist America*. Their analysis was the first I had seen that combined Leftist political understandings with educational theory and research, and it made me realize I, too, could link my political values with intellectual work. As soon as I finished my dissertation, I retooled. I called on my love of history and my previous experience in teaching and social movement organizing, and labored for almost a year on a long manuscript about U.S. history curriculum and the American working class. I sent it off to the *Harvard Educational Review* because of its reputation as "a journal that everyone read." I was sure that in ten months I would get a resounding rejection. One evening two or three weeks later I got a phone call telling me that they had accepted my work. But, the caller said, they were going out for pizza and would get back to me about some revisions they wanted. I was enthralled at the acceptance. But pizza! How could they think about pizza at a time like this?!

When the editors wrote up the changes they wanted, I was dismayed. It seemed they were asking for an entire rewrite. But, not wanting to miss the opportunity to publish in the *Review*, I toiled away, working closely with a member of the Editorial Board. Several months later I turned in a much-improved manuscript. During the entire time, I was sure they were going to change their minds and say they didn't want it after all! When the article appeared it was well received and allowed me to establish an initial presence in the field. I was pleased, and felt warmly toward the *Review*. I followed the journal over the years and watched as it published excellent articles. I was in good company! Recently, when the current editors asked me to contribute a piece on education policy for their anniversary issue, I was happy to do so. It felt like coming home.

Nelly P. Stromquist

The *Harvard Educational Review* entered into my consciousness a long time ago, when I became aware of two of its features: First, as a publication edited by students, it promised inherent vitality, hope, and assertiveness in the treatment of educational issues. Second, many of its articles have addressed issues through a clear philosophical lens — issues that have an impact on the betterment of society, such as the potential of education to transform economic and cultural contexts, social class and stratification, equality and equity policies, and student learning. Through many generations of Harvard education students, *HER* has managed to maintain its character as a journal of "opinion and research," dedicated to the presentation of high-quality research but not forgetting that research should guide action.

Kevin K. Kumashiro

In the mid-1990s, I began studying the intersections of race and sexuality in education. Very little had been published on the topic at that time, and while my mentors suggested that I could help to fill this gap, I remember feeling discouraged that, in the field of education, few leaders had taken the initiative to assert the importance of this area of research. Barely a year into my study, one friend after another sent me e-mail announcements about a special issue on gay, lesbian, bisexual, and transgender people in education published by one of the top educational research journals. I read the entire issue, rereading the articles at the intersection of race and sexuality, and felt all the more empowered in my work. If the *Harvard Educational Review* could produce this special issue, surely the time for my study had come.

Throughout my studies as a graduate student, my teaching in faculties of education, and my ongoing research, I have turned time and again to the *Harvard Educational Review* for groundbreaking works on social justice in the various disciplines in educational research, including many of the articles cited in the chapters of this volume. I have also turned to *HER* when looking for venues to publish research in which I try my hardest to go against the grain, whether it be research on the repetitions that hinder movements toward social justice in learning, teaching, supervising, and researching, or research that reflects collaboratively on the peer-review process for publishing in research journals. I have twice had the opportunity to work with members of the Editorial Board in significantly revising my writing, and I believe their editorial process models collaboration and collegiality. The *Harvard Educational Review* has positively influenced my research and my growth as a researcher, and I know I am not alone. I congratulate *HER* on its accomplishments, and I look forward to its next seventy-five years.

Notes on the Editors

MEGIN CHARNER-LAIRD is a doctoral candidate in Learning and Teaching at the Harvard Graduate School of Education. She conducts research for the Project on the Next Generation of Teachers, as well as the Urban Impact Project, of which she is a founding member. She is a current cochair of the *Harvard Educational Review* and a Spencer Research Training Grant recipient. A former elementary school teacher, Charner-Laird's research interests center around the preparation experiences of teachers and their ongoing development in the profession. She is particularly interested in the experiences of teachers in urban settings and is currently conducting a longitudinal study investigating the preparation and on-the-job experiences of teachers who were trained to enter urban schools.

MORGAEN L. DONALDSON is an advanced doctoral student at the Harvard Graduate School of Education, a researcher at the Project on the Next Generation of Teachers, and a Spencer Research Training Grant recipient. She is a coauthor of *Finders and Keepers: Helping New Teachers Survive and Thrive in Our Schools* (2004) and *Reflections of First-Year Teachers on School Culture: Questions, Hopes, and Challenges* (1999). A former high school teacher, Donaldson was a founding faculty member of the Boston Arts Academy, Boston's public high school for the arts. She studies teachers' career development, professional growth, and current changes in rural and urban schools.

SOO HONG is a doctoral candidate in Administration, Planning, and Social Policy at the Harvard Graduate School of Education and a Spencer Research Training Grant recipient. Her work focuses on the relationships between immigrant/refugee communities and schools and the possibilities for community and parent engagement. Hong has also conducted research for the Maryland State Department of Education and worked on the Harvard Immigration Project. Prior to her doctoral studies, she worked as an elementary and middle school teacher in Boston and Silver Spring, Maryland.

Guidelines for Authors

The *Harvard Educational Review* accepts contributions from teachers, practitioners, policymakers, scholars, and researchers in education and related fields, as well as from informed observers. In addition to discussions and reviews of research and theory, *HER* welcomes articles that reflect on teaching and practice in educational settings in the United States and abroad. Authors can elect to indicate whether they are submitting their manuscript as an article, a Voices Inside Schools article, an essay review, or a book review. *HER* has a two-stage review process. Manuscripts that pass the initial stage are then considered by the full Editorial Board and receive written feedback. It is the policy of the *Review* to consider for publication only articles that are not simultaneously being considered elsewhere. **Please follow these guidelines in preparing your manuscript for submission.**

1. Authors must submit three copies of the manuscript, including a one-page abstract. Manuscripts will be returned only if a stamped, self-addressed envelope is included at the time of submission. In addition, please include a clearly labeled 3.5-inch disk containing an electronic version of the manuscript in Microsoft Word format. If you do not have access to MS Word, please contact us to make other arrangements.

2. Manuscripts are considered anonymously. The author's name must appear *only* on the title page; any references that identify the author in the text must be deleted.

3. HER accepts manuscripts of **up to 15,000 words**, including footnotes and references, and reserves the right to return any manuscript that exceeds that length.

4. All text must be **double-spaced**, and type size must be at least **12 point with 1-inch margins on both sides**.

5. Quoted material is extracted in the text when it is more than 45 words, unless the editors determine otherwise.

6. Authors should refer to *The Chicago Manual of Style* for general questions of style, grammar, punctuation, and form. *Chicago* **should also be referred to for footnotes of theoretical, descriptive, or essay-like material**.

7. **For technical and research manuscripts, authors should use the *Publication Manual of the American Psychological Association* for reference and citations format.**

8. *The Uniform System of Citation,* published by the *Harvard Law Review,* should be used for articles that rely heavily on legal documentation. Because this form is not easily adaptable to other sources, it is usually combined with *The Chicago Manual of Style* as necessary.

9. Authors should select the style most suitable for their manuscripts and adhere consistently to that style. The Editors reserve the right to request that authors use

an alternative style if the one chosen seems inappropriate. Styles may not be combined, with the exception of legal citations.

10. **References must be in APA format.** We request that authors provide complete references, including page citations in book reviews. Authors should be certain that citations and footnotes in the text agree with those in the references.

11. As a generalist journal, *HER* discourages the use of technical jargon. We encourage authors to minimize the use of parentheses, italics, and quotation marks for emphasis in the text. Footnotes should be as few and as concise as possible. Tables and figures should be kept to a minimum.

Voices Inside Schools

The purpose of this section is to provide a forum devoted to the voices of teachers, students, and others committed to education within the school community broadly defined—psychologists, social workers, principals, counselors, librarians, and custodians, for example—who interact with students and who have important knowledge and expertise about life inside schools gained through practice, reflection, and/or research. We value the writing of adults and students who have intimate and first-hand experience with teaching and learning.

Submissions for the Voices Inside Schools section are written by teachers and other professionals in the field of education about their own practice, and by students about their own educational experiences. In the past, *HER* has published articles by practitioners on a wide variety of issues: a Black educator's experiences teaching writing as a process to minority students, a literacy educator teaching women in a correctional facility, a university professor describing the content and pedagogy of her course on AIDS, and a school principal reflecting on school restructuring. Authors may choose to present their perspective through a range of formats, from data-driven to more reflective essays.

Book Reviews

HER also accepts reviews of recent publications (within the last two years) about education. Book reviews, in which the author reviews a book related to education, should be 8–12 double-spaced pages. *HER* also publishes essay reviews, in which one or more books in a particular field are analyzed and the implications for future research and practice are discussed. These essays should range from 15–20 pages. More detailed guidelines for book and essay reviews are available from the *HER* office. Please call 617-495-3432, or write to the address below.

To submit a manuscript to the *Harvard Educational Review*, please send three double-spaced copies, with the author's name on the title page only, to:

Harvard Educational Review
Harvard Graduate School of Education
8 Story Street
Cambridge, MA 02138